Dr. Dorus Paul Rudisill is Professor of Philosophy and Religious Studies at Lenoir Rhyne College and Head of the Department.

Dr. Rudisill was born in Cherryville, North Carolina, and was educated at Lenoir Rhyne College, Lutheran Theological Southern Seminary, University of South Carolina, Hartford Seminary, and Duke University. Prior to this coming to Lenoir Rhyne College, he was minister to four Lutheran parishes in North Carolina. During his ministry he organized three congregations.

Dr. Rudisill has filled numerous appointments as lecturer and preacher during his years at Lenoir Rhyne College. He was a member of the Board of Trustees of the Lutheran Theological Southern Seminary for a number of years and served as a delegate to the National Council of Churches on two occasions.

The
Doctrine of The Atonement
in
Jonathan Edwards
and
His Successors

The Doctrine of The Atonement in Jonathan Edwards and His Successors

by

DORUS PAUL RUDISILL, PH.D.

Poseidon Books, Inc.
New York, N. Y.

First Edition

Library of Congress Catalog Card Number: 77-151509
SBN - 8181 - 9998 - 9

Published by Poseidon Books, Inc.
101 Fifth Avenue
New York, N. Y.

MANUFACTURED IN THE UNITED STATES OF AMERICA

TO THE MEMORY

OF

MY PARENTS

CONTENTS

CHAPTER 2—The Doctrine of The Atonement in Joseph Bellamy

CHAPTER 3—The Doctrine of The Atonement in Samuel Hopkins

CHAPTER 4—The Doctrine of The Atonement in Stephen West

PREFACE

THE CURRENT REVIVAL of interest in the Atonement makes it opportune to investigate a virgin area of thought on this important doctrine. Considerable attention has been paid to the doctrines of God and man in the writings of Jonathan Edwards and his successors. It is surprising to find that the doctrine of the Atonement by these theologians has received such scant attention.

Jonathan Edwards, Sr. (1703-1758) did not write a systematic treatise on the Atonement. He did develop and espouse a view that was new, although many elements in it had appeared previously. This doctrine was noticeably basic in his preaching. This novel doctrine had considerable influence especially on New England preaching during the latter part of the eighteenth century. It was his view that was largely responsible for the development of the Doctrine of the Atonement by his successors, who were known as the Edwardeans.

In this book, I shall cite Edwards' divergencies from the Penal Doctrine of the Atonement that was predominant at that time in New England. Also, I shall show that the Edwardean theory lay in the theory of Edwards, but contained some essential differences. The development of the doctrine of the Atonement by the Edwardeans, however, was influenced at a number of points by three New England preachers who formed a connecting link between Edwards and the Edwardeans. The doctrines of Joseph Bellamy (1719-1790), Samuel Hopkins (1721-1803), and Stephen West (1735-1816) forged this connecting link. Their modifications of Edwards' view will be stated. I shall state the doctrine of the Atonement as it was held by Jonathan Edwards, Sr., and show his influence upon the latterly developed Edwardean doctrine. Comparisons and contrasts among the views separately described will then be given.

I am deeply indebted to Dr. H. Sheldon Smith of Duke University for awakening my interest in New England theology of the eighteenth century. I also wish to express my gratitude to President Raymond M. Bost and Professor Ralph H. Lyerly, my colleagues at Lenoir Rhyne College, for their helpful suggestions in the preparation of this book.

Lenoir Rhyne College
Hickory, North Carolina

D. P. R.

INTRODUCTION

Christianity may be classified as a redemptive religion. Its uniqueness does not consist in this claim, for some other religions, too, have redemptive aspects. The uniqueness of Christianity is in the person and work of Jesus Christ. Thus the central problem in Atonement is that of relating Christ's redemptive acts to man's predicament as a sinner before God.

The essentials of Christian theology are two: revelation and reflection. Revelation is God's self-disclosure to sinful man with redemption in view. Revelation is not to be considered a disclosure that evokes an affirmation that there is a God; rather, that in God's redemptive acts is His self disclosure. Reflection is the analysis, interpretation, and correlation of the elements of revelation. Although reflection seeks to understand revelation, it is kept humble by its inability to plumb the profundity of God's self-disclosure.

Christ is the supreme revelation of God. This truth is the basic affirmation of Christian faith. Both sin and grace, both judgment and peace, are disclosed by Him. And the cross is more than a symbol of these paradoxes; it is the instrument of their reconciliation. The cross has been peculiarly fundamental in Christian faith and hope because the cross has been adjudged to be the quintessence of God's revelation to sin-laden humanity. Christ's suffering and death elicit repentance and effect peace and hope. This proclamation is the evangel that has been proclaimed by the Church. How His suffering and death are an atonement has been variously conceived. Reflection has yielded manifold results.

It was natural that inquiry arose as to the *modus operandi* of Christ's passion in effecting forgiveness and peace. It was natural that inquiry arose because the mind of man cannot remain quiescent when it is faced by such a glaring contradiction as that between the sufferings and sinlessness of Christ. His sinlessness has been affirmed by the Church. It is the *sine qua non* of every doctrine of the Atonement. If the sinless die in this manner, what must be believed about God? Does not this ironical end present an insistent problem about God's justice? However, the problem is increased by the affirmation of the resurrection, for Christ's death and resurrection have an inextricable affinity in Christian thought. The resurrection tells something new about the nature and significance of Christ's life and death. The chief contradiction about the death of the sinless Christ is found in the oft-repeated question: How is the horrible cross from which I would fain turn my face the very beginning and realization of a hitherto unexperienced peace and hope?

The question of *modus operandi* of redemption could not be evaded once the divinity of Jesus Christ was affirmed. The terrific fact of the universality of death has troubled the mind of man throughout recorded history and has evoked manifold explanations as to its place and significance in the universal scheme. But for incarnate Deity to die! That demands deeper analysis because of its sheer contradiction. And to add: He died for man or on account of man's sin! That provokes inquiry into the nature of sin and the necessity of Atonement. It provokes another question: How is the death of incarnate Diety related to the Christian experience of forgiveness and reconciliation? It may be confidently said that the theological problem involved in Christ's suffering and death is in direct ratio to the nature of Being ascribed to Him. Accordingly, the validity of redemption by Him has been grounded in the nature of His person. For this reason, questions about the nature of Christ and the Atonement have been fundamentally practical.

Four types of Atonement theories are discerned in the history of Christian thought: Ransom, Objective, Subjective, and Objective-Subjective. It should be explicitly stated that neither a critique of these theories nor a genetic history of the efforts which have been made to state a doctrine of the Atonement is being presented. It suffices for our present purpose to present the salient features of these types. (The value of this presentation will become apparent when the doctrine of the Atonement in Jonathan Edwards and his successors is critically examined.)

The Ransom theory presupposes a literal interpretation of New Testament passages that refer or allude to Christ's death as a ransom to the devil. This view holds that Christ paid a ransom in suffering and dying. It may be pointed out here that Aulen in his *Christus Victor,* strongly urges a reinterpretation of the Ransom idea. His book presupposes the objective reality of sin, death, and the devil. Thus, Christ's victory has meaning not only in reference to man's predicament as sinner but it also has a cosmic significance.

The Objective views presuppose that sin has involved man in a state of guilt that cannot be eradicated by man's repentance, even if full repentance were possible. Theories of this type also presuppose that God cannot forgive without some satisfaction being made to Him. That is to say, repentance cannot in and of itself eradicate the entail of guilt for sins; and forgiveness without satisfaction for sin is inconsistent with the nature of God as just and holy. Thus vicarious substitution is an inexorable element in strictly Objective theories.

The Subjective theories focalize God's benevolence, the cross being the expression of God's unutterable, forgiving love. This type urges that man's contrition for sins, renunciation of evil, and disavowal of allegiance to any other God than the Father of the Lord Jesus Christ is God's purpose through the cross. Vicarious satisfaction for Atonement is obviously denied by affirming the adequacy of man's responding faith and love for reconciliation.

Although one frequently finds the term "subjective" in presentation of the Penal theory, an Objective type, it is important to note that the subjective element, faith, is the apprehension of the benefits of the Atonement, objectively considered. "Subjective faith" does not connote the same thing as "Subjective Atonement." The former is the act of apprehending something done *ab extra*; the latter is Christ's act terminating upon man. The former relates to *Christus pro nobis;* the latter, to *Christus in nobis.*

The Objective-Subjective theories show that sin has caused mutual alienation between God and man, and that the Atonement must terminate upon both God and man. Objective Atonement signifies that something has been done toward God, such as satisfaction of his justice through the suffering of Christ, or satisfaction of his honor in lieu of suffering deserved by man. Atonement, being an *ab extra* transaction, is real, whether it is ever accepted by or made effective in any life. Subjective Atonement terminating upon man is accomplished when man is awakened to the heinousness of sin and to the boundless love of God for sinners. According to Objective-Subjective Atonement, neither the Objective nor the Subjective aspect is an Atonement in itself. Atonement is accomplished when these contrary aspects are present and united in such a manner as to make these aspects complementary.

It is convenient to catalogue theories according to the aforenamed types. The variations within these categories are numerous. It is not at all surprising that in the spate of soteriological writings we find so many and such wide divergences in views on the Atonement when we take into consideration that the doctrine of the Atonement both conditions and is conditioned by other doctrines in any system of theology. That is, the Atonement is not an isolated doctrine. It would be well to look hastily at a few of the major conditioning factors that account for the wide variety of views on the Atonement.

Assuming that the sacrificial system in the Old Testament is ordained of God and that its efficacy is not independent of but dependent upon the vicarious sacrifice of Christ, the death of Christ is viewed as the necessary fulfillment of the will and purpose of God in requiring sacrifices by the shedding of blood. Thus, the death of Christ as the only adequate sacrifice for sin validates its antetypes. All former sacrifices were mere adumbrations and therefore inefficacious without validation by the sacrifice of Christ. When Christ died, the entire sacrificial system was abrogated, its abolishment being a corollary of the adequacy of the death of the true Mediator. This inextricable relation between Old Testament blood sacrifices and the sacrifice of Christ is an indispensable presupposition. Examples are the Penal theory, an Objective type, and that of Jonathan Edwards, Sr.

Affirming the divinity of Christ, we inevitably see that great importance be assigned His suffering and His death. The phenomena of suffering and death in the world have given rise to various theories as to their origin and significance. And the enigma is deepened when it is affirmed that the God-man suffered and died. Was His passion because God's nature is such that He cannot consistently forgive man until satisfaction be made for insolent disobedience? Is the gravity of sin such that it requires so great an expiation? Or does His passion signify that man's heart is so calloused and darkened as to require so potent a provocation and illumination? Whatever the theory of the Atonement may be, if the divinity of Christ be affirmed, some momentous significance must be attached to His passion.

Disavowing the deity of Christ we cannot logically see in His passion an element of objectivity. He becomes humanity's peerless example of devotion to truth and duty. The unmerited pain and ignominy that He suffered at the hands of a mob is a frightful index to the capacity of sinful man to do evil. The efficacy of Jesus' life thus lies in its power to make man better. Jesus' suffering and death hauntingly accuse man: His life incites man to emulate the nobleness and disinterestedness which characterized Him; His triumph encourages man in the hope that to him the victory belongs. Specifically, the cogency of a sinless martyr's influence in evoking man's repentance and rectification is the force of the theory of Faustus Socinus.

A theologian's approach, whether philosophical or psychological, conditions his view. For example, Anselm, an extreme rationalist, develops his theory along *a priori* lines. He is concerned not with an examination of the Christian's experience of having been redeemed but with an exposition of the logical necessity for and sufficiency of the God-man for redemption. On the other hand, Rashdall and Mackintosh, two recent theologians, see no necessity for any *a priori* considerations. Instead they urge that ideas of the Atonement must stem from the experience of forgiveness and reconciliation. Obviously, views on the Atonement that stem from such different points of departure cannot coincide.

Varying views on anthropology will inevitably yield divergent theories of the Atonement. The conclusions of a liberal theologian who works within a framework of certain evolutionary views will not coincide with the opinions of theologians who labor within another context. In short, one's doctrines of God, the Trinity, the Scriptures, and man are important factors in any concatenation.

In the course of the discussion of Edwards' theory of the Atonement reference will be made to the Old New England view for the purpose of seeing to what extent Edwards' doctrine differs from it. A statement of the view held prior to and generally during Edwards' day, commonly referred to as the "Old New England View," should be given. That can be done briefly, for the Old New England View is neither an uncommon type of theory nor an uncommon theory. It is an objective view of the Atonement. Specifically, it is the Penal theory of Hyper-Calvinism which holds that Christ satisfied distributive justice by suffering both the precise quantity and the precise quality of punishment that the elect would have suffered throughout eternity if Christ had not suffered in their stead.

Chapter 1

THE DOCTRINE OF THE ATONEMENT IN JONATHAN EDWARDS, SR.

I. PRELIMINARY OBSERVATIONS

FOUR SIGNIFICANT OBSERVATIONS should be made before attention is concentrated upon Edwards' doctrine of the Atonement. The pertinence of these observations will become increasingly apparent as we critically examine the views that are discoverable in his *Works*.[1]

A. God as *Being in General*

THERE IS NOTHING distinctive about Edwards' pronouncements on the Trinity[2] and the two natures of Christ. He adheres to orthodox Calvinism at these points. However, his conception of God as *Being in general* should be noted together with its implications. He maintains that the existence of nothing is a rational absurdity. God is *Being in general.* It would be improper to say that God is *a* being for He is not a genus who can be particularized in species. To say that He is *a* being would infer the possibility of other beings, but God as Being implies that there is no other and that another Being could not exist.[3]

Edwards taught that the creation of the world and of intelligent beings is a divine necessity on account of the nature of *Being in general*.

God is perfect; He is the Ineffable Being. Being perfect actuality, He is disposed to emanate Himself, His effulgency by inner necessity expressing itself. Creation is not an act that was performed by fiat in the remote past; it is continuous, and the existence of created objects is not the ground or cause of their continued existence.

Moreover, qualities of matter are not resident in matter but in the mind. Matter apart from mind is the occasion for perceptive experience. Here his view coincides almost precisely with that of George Berkeley. Matter, or all things that we commonly speak of as tangible and visible, is the emanation of the natural attributes of God. It is important to note further that the moral attributes of God are emanated. Thus, there is emanation both with respect to God's natural attributes such as omnipotence and omnipresence and with respect to His moral attributes such as holiness and justice.

Edwards' teaching about personal identity derives from his doctrine of Being. By the will and appointment of God, the descendants of Adam are united with him to constitute one moral whole. It is in this concept of preservation that Edwards grounds the doctrine of original sin which will shortly demand our consideration.

Edwards' affirmation of God's self-love and absolute moral sovereignty stem from this conception of Being. Knowing Himself to be perfectly holy, He wills Himself as the end. His propensity to diffuse Himself has been noted. This propensity to diffuse Himself is also a propensity to Himself undiffused. That is to say, the will of God expresses itself both by emanation and remanation, both with respect to His natural and His moral attributes.[4]

Emanation-remanation as it is related to the moral attributes of God is specially relevant to our subject. Three aspects of this principle are to be noted. First, the source of emanation is God. There are no quiescent attributes in Him. His moral attributes must be expressed on account of His nature. Second, the content of emanation is the moral quality of God. It is spiritual understanding, holiness, and happiness. This moral quality was emanated to Adam at the creation. Humanity lost it by Adam's fall but the content of emanation is restored in regeneration. It will be important to bear this in mind when Edwards' doctrine of grace is being considered. Third, the end of emanation is God Himself. Emanation is reflected back to God in remanation. This is the core of Edwards' idea of virtue. To anticipate, virtue is disinterested benevolence. The glory of God "is both exhibited and acknowledged" in the "creature's knowing, loving, and rejoicing in and praising God." When the creature loves God supremely and makes His glory the primary purpose in life, there is *rapport* between God and man or between God's will toward Himself and man's toward God. Does man's refusal to reflect God's glory interrupt emanation-remanation? It does not. Here sovereign election enters into the matter. God elects those to whom an emanation of spiritual understanding, holiness, and happiness is given. They must remanate His emanation because grace is irresistible. Moreover, all God's attributes must be expressed. When He expresses His wrath in punishing the nonelect He is glorifying Himself. This, too, is emanation-remanation.

B. The Sovereignty of God

WE SHOULD OBSERVE, in the second place, Edwards' stress upon the sovereignty of God. He holds that "the sovereignty of God is his absolute independent right of disposition of all creatures according to his own pleasure."[5] In his first printed sermon, *God Glorified in the Work of Redemption by the Greatness of Man's Dependence upon Him in the Whole of It,*[6] Edwards champions the doctrine of God's sovereignty. But emphasis upon sovereignty is the common possession of all Calvinists!

Why is it important to single out Edwards as an exponent of this doctrine? Two reasons are apparent. First, New England Calvinism prior to 1730 had been modified by such alien elements as Stoddardeanism and the Half-Way Covenant and New England preaching had abandoned to a considerable extent the citadel of sovereignty in the face of the siege of Arminianism. Edwards endeavored to re-establish Calvinism. His grandfather, Solomon Stoddard, minister of Northampton, Massachusetts (1669-1729), was the innovator in 1707 of what became known as Stoddardeanism, namely that the unconverted should be given the privilege of the Lord's Supper on the ground that it was a converting ordinance. This practice marked a leniency that was not allowed even in the Half-Way Covenant, which in itself was a departure from New England Calvinism. Formerly only baptized Christians who had experienced a spiritual illumination were permitted to present their children for baptism. The Half-Way Covenant allowed parents who had been baptized but who did not profess conversion to have their children baptized.

These baptized but "nonregenerated" Christians were not privileged to receive the Lord's Supper. Thus, the church privileges of the nonregenerate were limited to a single sacrament and to the disciplinary oversight of the church. These practices together with Arminian stress upon freedom of the will had vitiated Calvinistic preaching.

The second reason for this consideration of Edwards' view of sovereignty is its connection with the Atonement. Edwards exalts the sovereignty of God with respect to the Atonement by giving a prominence to God as a Sovereign in applying and conducting as well as in originating the redemptive work.

The significant fact to note is neither that God originates redemption nor that redemption is effected by Him; these emphases are the common possession of virtually all writers on the Atonement. The point to be stressed is that God is sovereign in "applying and conducting" redemption. He is sovereign in the matter of election and imputation.

Edwards' supralapsarian view of election may be stated briefly as follows: election is the predetermined and inviolate decree of the inscrutable will of the sovereign God respecting every soul He creates. Edwards does not distinguish between the foreknowledge and foreordination of God. God foreknows and foreordains all things. His omniscience and prescience are minutely perfect.[7]

Regarding predestination, however, there is this distinction: from eternity God decreed the election of discrete souls, but He did not decree the damnation of nameable or identifiable individuals.[8] From eternity God ordained the salvation of the elect, determining the exact number and the specific persons to be saved. The Atonement was posited on this absolute foreknowledge and foreordination. It was not in the least dissipated on the condemned,[9] for Christ did not suffer for them. Therefore it was a Limited Atonement. The damned never rejected the benefit of Christ's work of redemption because it was not effectively proffered to them.

It could not be proffered to them because Christ did not take upon Himself their sins. And He did not take upon Himself their sins because they were not among the elect.[10] This conception of a Limited Atonement correlates with another element in his doctrine, that grace is always morally efficacious.[11] The sovereign will of God cannot be hindered, and His sovereign grace cannot become ineffective. Moreover, God's inscrutable will to save the elect is revealed only as God has chosen to disclose it. The disclosure of His will of election is the complement to the experience of redemption by the elect. It is only as God speaks and acts that His will is known and it is only as an experient is being acted upon that the sovereign will for that person is disclosed. This accounts for Edwards' great care and fervor in preaching for it is through universal proclamation that God's efficacious grace becomes known and effective in whomsoever He has elected.[12]

C. Forensic Framework

The third observation is that Edwards' doctrine of the Atonement is cast for the most part in a forensic framework. Since this is the case we should inquire into Edwards' idea of law and justice.

The divine law is comprehended in the command to love.[13] In terms suitable to Edwards' idea of Being, the command should be stated thus: Thou shalt possess disinterested benevolence for *Being in general* and express true benevolence to every intelligent being in exact ratio to the amount of being each possesses. The antipode of this is self-love which manifests itself in hatred of God and one's neighbor.[14]

It is not necessary for our present purpose to discuss this tenet but it is necessary to raise the question as to the arbitrariness of the law. Edwards' successors conceived of law as a transcript of God; that is, law is the *sine qua non* of moral relationship between the Governor and His subjects and its nature derives from the nature of God. Therefore, it is never merely arbitrary. Edwards maintains that the commands and prohibitions of God are only significations of our duty and of his nature,[15] implying that the law is not an arbitrary inhibition of man's freedom but that it is an inherent corollary of being in relationship with God. This implication is sustained by an examination of Edwards' *The Nature of True Virtue*.[16]

The essence of true virtue is disinterested benevolence. God's command to man is comprehended in love. Love which does not make God its sole object is not pure. The presence of any selfish interest in one's love for God is sure evidence that God is not the sole object. For example, he is selfishly concerned who loves God in the hope of enjoying the blessings of heaven as a reward. God must be loved for what He is in Himself and not for any reward of blessing one may hope to receive from Him or even from the experience of loving Him. With respect to one's loving his fellow-creatures, disinterested benevolence means that they are to be loved in God. In other words no creature is to be loved or honored on account of what he is in himself, regardless of his character or station in life. Although the Biblical command to love is twofold, in actuality true love for one's neighbor is love for *Being in general*. If a person makes another person the real object of his love he is as guilty of idolatry as if he bowed to a pagan idol. Thus the essence of true virtue is disinterested benevolence because it makes *Being in general*, or God, the end.[17] Since God loves Himself supremely and wills Himself as the end, He wills that His intelligent creatures love Him supremely, undividedly, and disinterestedly. Because the end of the law is the same as the end of God's will for Himself, the law is a transcript of Himself. When His will, which is His law, is supremely regarded by man there is perfect rapport between God and man. This, in one respect, is emanation-remanation.

It would be correct to affirm that the law is not an arbitrary contrivance. However, three aspects of Edwards' thought need to be introduced here. First, it is clearly taught by him that God decrees sin and punishment.[18] This sovereign decree does not alter God's inexorable will about Himself as the end nor does it alter His command that disinterested benevolence be perfectly expressed in the lives of all intelligent creatures. Edwards distinguishes between God's will of command and His will of decree.[19] His will of command is primary. He wills Himself as the end and He wills that the entire intelligent creation will Him as the end. His will of decree is not secondary in the sense that it is less important, but it is secondary in the sense that it is an instrumental, functional will. His will of decree is consonant with His will of command. Thus, by decreeing sin and punishment, God's will of command is glorified. If His will of decree had not been expressed—that is, if sin and punishment were unknown phenomena—God's awful majesty, His authority, dreadful greatness, justice, and holiness would not be manifest. But the manifestation of these attributes is indispensable for His will of command about Himself as the end. Furthermore, Edwards maintains that God wills what is contrary to excellency in some particulars for the sake of a more general excellency and order.[20]

In the second place, Edwards' distinction between God's obligation to fulfill a threatening and His obligation to fulfill a promise should be noted. He holds that the obligation to fulfill a threatening does not result from the threatening itself; that is, the obligation to fulfill a threatening is not a consequence of the threatening *as a threatening,* for threatening inheres in God's will of command. It is not consequent upon nor subsequent to His will of command. On the other hand, the obligation to fulfill a promise does result in part from the promise itself. That is to say there is an indispensable element of gratuity in God's promise. But once the promise is made, God obligates Himself to fulfill that promise.[21]

Since the obligation to fulfill the threatening is absolute and not in any measure consequent upon the threatening as a threatening, a *quid pro quo*[22] view of Christ's satisfaction is an ineluctable corollary. Edwards' successors, notably Emmons and Griffin, did not accept this distinction between an obligation to fulfill a threatening and an obligation to fulfill a promise. Their views will be examined later in Chapter V of this study. It is sufficient here to point out that by seeing the obligation to fulfill a threatening as depending upon the threatening itself they were able consistently to abandon all semblance of a *quid pro quo* idea of the Atonement.

Also, it will be shown in this present chapter (under the discussion of Adam's pristine state) that Edwards maintains that if Adam had kept God's law his obedience would not have merited God's rewarding him. Conversely, Adam's failure to keep God's law issued in condign punishment. Furthermore, Edwards does not so much as intimate that it was the divine will that Adam and his posterity should have remained sinless. On the contrary the fact of sin is empirical proof that God willed sin. Sin was ordained as a contrivance by means of which His attributes of mercy and vindictive justice might be displayed. All facets of God's nature could not have been made known to His intelligent creatures without the display of these attributes.[23]

Thus, Edwards grounds law in the holy and benevolent character of God. It is not arbitrary as such. However, it is affirmed that God decrees sin and according to His inscrutable will elects some souls for redemption and passes by other souls whose claim upon His mercy is no less deserving. That is equal to a declaration of sovereign discrimination. It does not temper the matter to say that His will is inscrutable. Obviously, neither the nature of God nor His total will is comprehended by man. To affirm the incomprehensibility of God and His will is quite a different matter from holding that God practices discrimination. If God decrees sin and elects some souls for redemption from the threatening penalty of the law, the law becomes subservient to His sovereign will. A serious implication of Edwards' view is the undermining of moral agency.

Since Edwards' doctrine of the Atonement is placed in a legal framework, it would be well to distinguish three types of justice: commutative, distributive, and general or public. These three types are to be found respectively in Anselm's *Cur Deus Homo,* the Penal view in Protestant Scholasticism, and the Edwardean theory during the latter part of the eighteenth century. Edwards himself works within both the commutative and distributive frameworks. This accounts, in part, for his lack of clarity at many points. He makes of Christ's satisfaction both the payment of a debt which merits a reward (commutative justice) and an expiation which forms the basis for the forensic justification of the sinful elect (distributive justice). It is not difficult to select excerpts which, if taken by themselves, point indisputably towards Edwards' adoption of the Anselmic theory or the Penal theory of orthodox Protestantism.[24]

Again, however, Edwards' stress upon sovereignty enters. This tends to disrelate Christ's work to justice in any form. The justification for this assertion lies in the fact that imputation is represented as an arbitrary act of sovereignty. This point will be elaborated later in this chapter.

It is not without significance that Edwards sporadically speaks of God as the Supreme Ruler whose relation to man is that of a ruler or governor to his subjects.[25] However, he does not explicitly affirm at any place that Christ satisfied general or public justice. Taken by themselves these rectoral representations are too infrequent to be of great weight in determining Edwards' view of the Atonement. It should be recalled, however, that Edwards read in manuscript Joseph Bellamy's *True Religion Delineated* (1750) without demurring to the latter's rectoral or governmental view, according to which Christ satisfied public or general justice and proffered salvation to everyone on the condition of faith. It should be recalled further that Edwards' untimely death in 1758 precluded his writing a new history of redemption which he had planned to do on a grand scale.[26] It is conjectural that this proposed work was to have been merely an elaboration of his *History of the Work of Redemption* which was written in 1739. What, if any, new ideas he wished to introduce about the Atonement, what old ideas he planned to abandon, he failed to tell us. The clue is not found in his later writings. When comparing these with Edwards' earlier writings one fails to discern a change in point of view. Thus too much importance must not be given to these infrequent rectoral references. Since his successors, the Edwardeans, adopted the rectoral framework, it is well to point out that there are occasional implications of it in Edwards' writings.

D. The Atonement Theory—Not an Issue

The final observation is that the Atonement was not a theological issue in New England during Edwards' ministerial career. Opportunity for the articulation of his polemic predilection was afforded by other issues.[27] Regarding the Atonement, Edwards did not attack any view presented by a then living theologian nor was he attacked by any contemporary New England Calvinist for his view. The former indicates that the Atonement was not then a current issue. The latter signifies that the divergence of Edwards' doctrine from the orthodox view of New England was not marked enough to demand a rebuttal, if a divergence were noticed at all. This is noteworthy. It indicates that he was thinking independently. Was he laying a foundation for his successors in deviating from the Old New England View on the Atonement? This is a major question in this book.

II. EDWARDS' DOCTRINE OF REDEMPTION

A. Historically Considered

EDWARDS' DOCTRINE OF the Atonement cannot be dissociated with impunity from his total view of redemption. It is imperative that the doctrine of the Atonement be placed in its soteriological context. There is a second reason for doing this. Edwards' views on the Atonement are pivotal. It will be profitable to have this broad perspective in mind when the views of his successors are examined.

Since Edwards' view of the economy of salvation is traced chronologically by him it is proper that his view of redemption be presented here historically. Also it appears to be the logical manner of presentation because the historical approach is the framework for the presentation of soteriological ideas. According to Edwards there is a markedly close relationship between the manifold acts of God. Each of God's acts is consistent with His own sovereign purpose and all

His sovereign purpose suffuses each sovereign act. Incidentally, Edwards' soteriological scheme is his philosophy of history.

B. Adam's Fall Involved Mankind in Sin

THE FIRST CONSIDERATION in an analysis of Edwards' doctrine of salvation is that of the original state of man. Adam was created in the image of God. This image was twofold: a moral or spiritual image and a natural image.[28] Being in harmonious relationship with his Creator, Adam's will had not been prejudiced by sinful desires nor had sin vitiated the proper motivation of acts towards the Lawgiver and the inviolate law under which the first man was placed. In his pristine state his will was unprejudiced.[29] It was *en rapport* with the will of God.

As a probationer, Adam was given two alternatives, a blessing and a curse. Eternal life was the proffered blessing, but this promise was made on the condition of obedience.[30] When Adam was created he was not justified, for he had not kept God's law. Since the promise was given conditionally, he was not then the recipient of God's full favor. He could justify himself by persevering in obedience.[31] But even so the bestowment of the blessing would be an act of sovereign grace. Adam was under a debt to the law of God, the keeping of which did not put the Creator under any obligation to bestow eternal life upon the created. The primacy and absoluteness of God's sovereignty is affirmed at this point and at every other point in Edwards' systematization of the economy of salvation.

In giving the law, God forewarned Adam that infraction of it would bring infinite guilt and unspeakably severe punishment. Here as elsewhere in Edwards' scheme the ratio of guilt corresponds to the amount of Being possessed by the person dishonored. Accordingly, the ratio of love must correspond to the amount of Being possessed by an intelligent person. God as *Being in general,* or possessing the most Being, demands and deserves perfect or disinterested benevolence. Correspondingly, sin against God is infinitely grievous and unspeakably heinous.[32]

When Adam fell by an act of disobedience, God validated His threatening by pouring out His vial of wrath upon the first man. Moreover, Adam's sin was not private although it was personal. In Adam all died. Suffering, death, and all mundane evils entered into the world on account of his sin. Edwards denies that original sin is a taint that is handed down from parent to child, a view which is consonant with traducianism. Creationism is affirmed. How Edwards relates each individual's sin to Adam's will be shown shortly. Humanity lost the moral but not the natural image on account of his sin. Henceforth man possesses natural ability but moral inability to do God's will. This is the basic position in Edwards' doctrine of freedom of the will.

Sin is never a state or condition. It is always an act or choice of will. This is extremely significant. This doctrine of original sin is rooted in his metaphysics. The propensity of man to sin; the propensity of unrestrained man to great wickedness; man's derogation of virtue and true religion; the presence of disease, suffering, and physical catastrophes; the depotentialization of the earth; and the universality of death are evidences of the universality of sin. The frightfulness of these phenomena lies in the fact that God's withdrawing Himself is the cause of them.[33] Parenthetically, cause and effect are always united in Edwards' scheme and God is always the efficient cause.

C. God's Work of Redemption

WRETCHED AND HELPLESS is man. The law is honorable and must be honored. Deference to the law is impossible so long as man is not repentant. If repentance were possible it would not erase the indelible stain of sin nor remove its guilt.[34] There is no remission of sin without satisfaction. The full need of punishment rests upon guilty man. There is no surcease from God's judgment if man be left to himself. But God Himself intervenes. To consummate His sovereign purpose for the elect, God becomes the originator and finisher of their salvation.

Our attention must now be given to God's "contrivance"[35] for the elect's redemption. There are two distinct but inseverable phases of redemption which are centered in Christ: the anticipatory and preparatory phase before His incarnation, and the phase beginning with the incarnation of Christ and culminating in His death, resurrection, and eternal reign. "The work of REDEMPTION is a work that God carries on from the fall of man to the end of the world."[36] The work of redemption in the former phase began immediately following the fall and continued uninterruptedly throughout that period of religious history covered by the Old Testament. It is the record of God's economy in bringing to fruition His purpose of redemption. The preservation of His chosen people throughout all their vicissitudes of fortune, the selection and preservation of the line from which the Messiah should come, the giving of the Decalogue and ceremonial laws, the provision of the sacrificial system, the appearance of antetypes of the Saviour in eminent figures, the quickening of hope of redemption, the writing of the Scriptures, and the disciplining of His people through captivities and privations were separate but not disjoined acts in the plan of redemption. All of this was preparatory and anticipatory. Although the Son who was to become incarnate was eminently present and active during this period, His efficacious work was futuristic. The redemptive scheme in the Old Testament was posited upon Christ's future sacrifice which was to validate its antetypes.[37]

"In the fulness of time God sent forth His Son." Edwards says that the Redeemer as the perfect Intercessor must have affinity with both God and man, must have a sympathetic understanding of each party and must be such a person as to deserve the respect and confidence of both parties. He must therefore be able to appraise the heinousness of sin from the divine point of view and be able to render adequate honor to God's law. On the other hand he must be in hearty sympathy with man and must be placed under the law to suffer the penalty for sin. The God-man was able to meet all requisites for man's salvation.[38]

He bore suffering incurred by man's infraction of the law. God visited upon Jesus Christ the full penalty that was due to man. God dealt with Him not as His Son but *as if* He were His *enemy*. The suffering of Christ was unspeakably severe, the severity of which is not to be adjudged solely by the excruciating pain He bore but by the anguish of His sinless soul.[39]

Edwards, in *Wisdom Displayed in Salvation,* holds that the majesty of God is exalted by the suffering of Christ. It is especially important to state this aspect of his view for it becomes prominent in the writings of his successors. It is important for the same reason to observe that the utterness, the abjectness of suffering in the death of Christ is adjudged to be the most cogent deterrent to sin, for in the death of God's beloved Son the unswerving determination of God to punish sin to the limit was manifest.[40] However, it is important to point out that Edwards holds that the pains of Christ were mere pains without any moral quality. Thus Edwards gives a new connotation to equivalence. The substitution of Christ was primarily in His heart.

This distinguishing feature of Edwards' theory should be underscored. The Penal theory stresses an equivalence between Christ's suffering and the suffering deserved by the human race, or by the elect where a Limited Atonement is held. Since Christ's substitution was primarily in His heart—the stress upon an equivalence of pain being abandoned—and since the pains were mere pains without a moral quality, Edwards' theory is widely divergent from that of his Calvinistic progenitors. Nevertheless, this modification is not tantamount to an abandonment of the notion of *quid pro quo* or distributive justice.

Edwards affirmed that Christ suffered the wrath of God in such a way as he was capable of. The context of this affirmation by Edwards is illuminating, for Edwards affirms that Christ knew that God was not angry with Him personally. Christ's suffering was not an experience of divine wrath such as the damned will experience in hell for they will be awesomely aware of God's wrathful hate.[41]

The significant implication of the affirmation that "Christ suffered as He was capable of" is that the nature of the God-man, while limiting the range of His experience in some respects, broadens that range in other respects. The vindictive justice of God is not tempered. Its frightful relentlessness is magnified because the utterness of God's wrath against sin was spilled upon His only beloved Son.[42] As the God-man the depth of His experience was increased. This is Edwards' point of view: because He was the God-man He could experience a suffering far deeper than the suffering the elect as mere human beings could possibly have experienced. This is what constitutes the superlative excellence of the substitution of Christ, a substitution that was primarily in His heart. And this capacity for deeper suffering is the real meaning of "as He was capable of."

It is scarcely possible for one to magnify and glorify the suffering of Christ more than Edwards does. The serious implication in this depiction arises from his explicit affirmation of Christ's suffering as the effect of His Father's vindictiveness. The avenging justice of God is put in high relief. Incidentally, Bellamy, Hopkins, West, and the exponents of the Edwardean theory of the Atonement follow Edwards' example in magnifying and glorifying the vindictive justice of God. It is an attribute that must be expressed since all attributes of God are functional.

D. Christ's Love for the Elect

EDWARDS LAYS SPECIAL stress upon Christ's great love for the elect. It was love that caused Him to come under the penalty of the law. Love motivated His suffering and death. Love led Him to earn a title to the elect's reward. Love will consummate their salvation because it will cause Him to be the elect's eternal surety and intercessor. The love of Christ is put in high relief.[43]

Parenthetically, the opposition of the Father's justice to the Son's love presents a problem for an advocate of the doctrine of the Trinity. The doctrine of the Trinity must be both moral and coherent. If Christ be the perfect revelation of God, the attributes which He manifested cannot stand in opposition to the attributes of His Father. If the doctrine of the Trinity be held, it must be insisted upon that love must be as prominent an attribute of the Father as of the Son, and justice must be as prominent an attribute of the Son as of the Father. It may be argued that the contrarity of justice and love is removed by the doctrine of Christ's humiliation. We shall see shortly that Edwards holds that a real option to obey or disobey was placed before Christ while He was performing His mediatorial mission and that God's sovereignty in and over Christ's life actually kept Christ from sinning. This only serves to increase the problem by injecting a Christological issue. If Christ completely emptied Himself of divinity, how can His suffering and death satisfy distributive justice for the elect and His obedience entitle them to a reward? If He did not empty Himself of divinity, why was the sovereignty of God in and over His life indispensable to His faithfulness unto death?

From the practical point of view, the opposition of God's justice against Christ's love accounts for the impression which has been widespread in Christianity: Christ is compassionate and therefore more approachable by the burdened soul than the Father who is uncompromisingly severe in His justice.

E. Christ Under Law

CHRIST HONORED THE law by a life of perfect obedience. He became subject to the moral law as a man, to the ceremonial law as a Jew, and to the mediatorial law as the Mediator.[44] Failure to keep the law would have wrought His eternal and irremediable undoing since there was no possible way by which He could have been redeemed. He could jusitfy Himself as an individual and as man's surety only by a life of perfect obedience. He did this. The inviolate sovereignty of God in and over Christ's life, Edwards declares, was responsible for the unsullied obedience of the Redeemer. Christ's obedience was complete and acceptable unto God, the resurrection attesting this fact.[45]

F. Forgiveness and Bestowment of Reward

EDWARDS DISTINGUISHES BETWEEN suffering and obedience as aspects of Christ's work of redemption, and relates these two aspects respectively to the elect's need for forgiveness of sins and to the bestowment of the reward of eternal life upon them. Nonimputation of guilt to the elect and imputation of righteousness to them are the respective complements of Christ's suffering and of his obedience.

It is important to observe that two lines of thought run parallel throughout Edwards' scheme of salvation. One line involves the sin of man, his guilt before the law, Christ's satisfaction of the threatened penalty of the law through suffering, and the nonimputation of guilt upon the elect for Christ's sake. This redemptive act is merely restorative to the pristine state, a state of probation.[46]

Mere restoration is inadequate for man's salvation. Man needs to be justified as well as restored. Closely complementary is a second line of thought: man's need of eternal life which could be bestowed only after God's law had been honored by obedience to it, the honoring of the law by Christ's obedience and the imputation of righteousness for Christ's sake.[47] These two lines converge in Christ, who is man's perfect surety.

It is obvious that Edwards views the work of redemption as a satisfaction of both distributive and commutative justice, the Penal and the Anselmic ideas respectively. By suffering, Christ satisfied distributive justice; by obedience, He satisfied commutative justice. The former is expiatory and the latter purchases a "title" to the elect's happiness and makes it "fit" that they receive the reward.[48]

Two important observations must not be overlooked. Edwards regards both the suffering and the humiliation of

Christ as constituting satisfaction for sin. Christ was bearing the penalty of the law even when He was not dying and when He was not experiencing physical pain, for example in the humble circumstances of His birth and the rest of His body in the tomb. This is extremely important because here Edwards removes the stress upon physical pain and emphasizes that Christ's satisfaction was primarily in His own heart. This is important also because Edwards maintains that His suffering and obedience cannot be dissociated morally, although they can be distinguished mentally.[49]

The second observation is a corollary. Although it is correct to distinguish between Christ's suffering and His obedience, it is imperative that we do not think of these aspects of His work as passive obedience and active obedience respectively. Edwards rejects this distinction, which was an important element in the Penal theory of orthodox Protestantism. Edwards' stress upon the voluntariness of Christ's submission to suffering, a moral act of obedience to the Father's will, makes of Christ's passion a moral act. It makes it active obedience.[50]

How does the work of Christ accrue to the favor of the elect? Edwards' answer is: "WE ARE JUSTIFIED ONLY BY FAITH IN CHRIST, AND NOT BY ANY MANNER OR VIRTUE OR GOODNESS OF OUR OWN."[51] This phraseology is old. Edwards put a unique interpretation upon it.

There is nothing distinctive about his definition of justification. It is a forensic term that refers to God's act of declaring a person righteous for Christ's sake.

It is not necessary to elaborate this point. Just one thing further needs to be said: according to Edwards, moral character and deserts are in no way transferable.

G. The Meaning of Faith

WITH RESPECT TO faith, Edwards uses the term in both a general and a specific sense. The general meaning of faith does not need to be stated. It is his understanding of "justifying faith" that calls for analysis. Justifying faith, or faith strictly considered, is a *vinculum*. It is that without which union between Christ and the believer cannot exist. Precisely speaking, it cannot be said that faith is that "by means of which" or "on account of which" union is effected because that puts too much strain upon the instrumentality of faith and upon man as the actor. The instrumentality of faith is not rejected nor is man's passivity affirmed, but God's efficacious grace in giving faith to the elect and Christ's activity in uniting Himself to man are kept in the foreground.[52]

It is important to stress that faith is not awakened in the soul by the knowledge of Christ's life and death. Simply considered faith is not the result of preaching or of sacred knowledge. However much a person may know about the Scriptures and assent to their teachings, however diligent he may be about worship and prayer, however strictly his life may adhere to the commandments of God and however much he may desire justifying faith—faith comes to whomsoever God wills to elect. Although one resolves to press into the Kingdom, or resolves as did Ruth to cleave only to God, there is no assurance that God will infuse grace or (which is the same thing) establish justifying *unition* (Edwards' oft-used term) between Christ and that soul.[53]

Faith is not a subjective apprehension of an objective merit. It is not an appropriation of the proffered boon. It is not an acceptance of an *ab extra* Atonement. It is a *vinculum*, a spiritual tie, a principle or quality of union between Christ and the elect. On account of His great *love* for the elect

Christ united Himself with them. Uniting Himself with them He took upon Himself their suffering lot. He came under the penalty of law. Now His coming under the penalty of the law because of a spiritual union is not the same thing as His taking upon Himself man's demerits and the punishment man deserved. The latter implies transfer, a view that is rejected.

Edwards avoids saying that God punished His son. Christ never stands outside of this spiritual union with the elect. Uniting Himself with the elect He took it upon Himself to purchase a "title" to their reward. It is by this union—in this union—that the elect receive forgiveness of sins and the reward. Christ is their patron, they are His clients. They are accepted into God's favor because the dignity of Christ's person and the Father's great love for His Son commend them to God's favor. Here we see Edwards' idea of merit as commendation or influence.[54] The elect stand within Christ's halo. They enjoy a reflected favor. The merit of Christ as a moral quality is not transferred to them nor strictly speaking is it adjudged to belong to them. There is no sweet exchange of sinner and Redeemer. Faith is a *vinculum*. By faith, the elect are beneficiaries of the favor that Christ merits for them. Unless one keeps in mind this union by faith between Christ and the elect he will misinterpret Edwards' use of "fitness," "qualification," "meetness" and "inherent goodness." It is by all of these that he explains the meaning of justification by faith alone.

It is instructive to note in this connection that Edwards so evaluates the merits of Christ—merits viewed as a moral quality—as to make it mandatory that those who have faith shall be rewarded.

However, it must be said that, according to Edwards, God's obligation is grounded in His sovereign promise to save the elect, a gratuitous promise which binds the veracity of God.

Therefore His soverignty is not impugned but glorified by the elect's claim.

H. Faith's Relation to Atonement

How is Edwards' doctrine of faith related to the Atonement? It is related in two ways. First, in the preliminary remarks on sovereignty it was shown that he considers imputation an act of sovereignty.

Second, faith is a *sine qua non* of Atonement because faith indicates a remanation of God's emanation. Christ's Atonement was not an *ab extra* transaction. It was a contrivance in sovereign prospect of the elect's salvation. It is conceivable, according to the strictly objective view of the atonement, that Christ's satisfaction of justice be a complete and adequate *ab extra* transaction without its being accepted or appropriated by any man. Not so by Edwards! God wills that specific souls be ultimately saved. His sovereign grace effects their faith and consequently His rewarding them. The visible work of Christ and His invisible voluntary substitution are expressions and evidences of God's propensity to emanate Himself. But emanation must be complemented by remanation. When emanation is expressed and evidenced through Christ it must evoke remanation from the elect. In the fact that only the elect through divine illumination see the dimension of sin in the Cross and abhor and abjure evil, and in the fact that through divine illumination only the elect see the beauty and symmetry of God and appreciate Him and cleave disinterestedly to Him alone, the Atonement is complete. The Atonement by Christ is not thereby emptied of some of its adequacy or meritoriousness. It is enhanced and glorified by its being so efficacious for the elect. Atonement is one aspect of emanation-remanation.

Finally, it may be noted that Edwards' depiction of Christ's work of redemption is, at places, reminiscent of the imagery common in the Patristic period: Christ is absolutely victorious. He overcomes Satan.

Chapter 2

THE DOCTRINE OF THE ATONEMENT IN JOSEPH BELLAMY

I. BELLAMY'S AFFILIATION WITH EDWARDS

JOSEPH BELLAMY WAS born in 1719 at New Cheshire, Connecticut and was graduated from Yale in 1735. He was a pupil and intimate friend of Jonathan Edwards, Sr. Following his ordination, he served as minister of the Congregational Church at Bethlem, Connecticut from 1740 until his death in 1790. He was both a renowned preacher and teacher. Jonathan Edwards, Jr. and John Smalley, two advocates of the Edwardean theory of the Atonement, were among his many pupils. Bellamy was closely associated with Samuel Hopkins for many years. His place as a connecting link between Jonathan Edwards, Sr. and his successors, known as the Edwardeans, is historically important, and his contributions to the Edwardean theory of the Atonement are weighty and significant.

II. BELLAMY'S DOCTRINE

A. Necessity for Atonement

Two apparent and significant deviations from Edwards' views should be noted immediately. Both of them were highly influential in the development of the Edwardean theory by Bellamy's pupils and their colleagues. First, Bellamy adopts the governmental or rectoral framework in accordance with which he maintains that Christ satisfied public or general justice in contradistinction to commutative and distributive justice. Correlatively, he holds that the doctrine of General Atonement rather than Limited Atonement is consistent with the teachings of Scripture. Edwards, as we have seen, holds Limited Atonement.

Special attention will be given to these two divergencies. While pursuing his development of these two innovations, we shall discern some other divergencies of a minor nature from Edwards' views.

Bellamy maintains that the Atonement was necessary on three counts. First, man stands in an inexcusable, condemned position before God who is the Moral Governor of the universe. God, according to His nature as the Sovereign Governor, has given His law under which man stands responsible to obey. Man has flouted the law by showing insolent disrespect for it. Consequently, he is under condemnation and in a state of callousness toward the Moral Governor and His law. Second, the Moral Governor would not be consistent with His own nature and with the nature of the law if He forgave sinners without having made a satisfaction which would render honor to the majesty of His Moral Government. Forgiveness without a satisfaction would tend to dishonor both the law and the Lawgiver since forgiveness without satisfaction would not display His determination to punish man for infractions. Third, Bellamy urges that it was necessary for God to send a Mediator through whom due satisfaction could be made and on whose account the Holy Spirit could act efficaciously in bringing the elect to the rewards of salvation.[1]

B. Three Essential Propositions

Bellamy states three propositions from which his entire view of the Atonement is deducted. The first proposition is stated in his *Works* as follows:

> The great God, the Creator, Preserver, Lord, and Governor of the world, is an absolutely perfect, an infinitely glorious and amiable Being, the supreme good, infinitely worthy of supreme love and honour, and universal obedience from His creature man.[2]

The fundamental nature of this proposition is apparent. There are, nevertheless, three pertinent observations to be made here.

First, Bellamy says that God's acts derive from the nature of His person. They are self-moved.

Second, Bellamy affirms that God loves to act like Himself. His acts are an expression of Himself. God acted like Himself in the Atonement. It was His act of infinite love or mercy. The Atonement was not an act that effected an alteration of His attitude toward man.

Third, Bellamy grounds his doctrine of disinterested benevolence in God's Being. Edwards, as has been pointed out, also derives disinterested benevolence from God as Being.

Bellamy's second basic proposition is expressed thus:

> The divine law, which requires this (universal obedience) of us, on pain of eternal death, is holy, just and good, a glorious law, worthy to be magnified and kept in honour in God's government.[3]

Divine law is the norm of relationship between God and all intelligent creatures. It is grounded in His very nature as holy, just, and good. God wills the law because it is right. The rightness of the law is not determined by any moral standard external to God's own nature. It derives from the inherent moral quality of the Lawgiver. God acts consistently with His own moral perfection in any relationship into which He enters, and He requires a corresponding excellence from the other party to that relationship. His moral perfection is comprehended in His holiness, which is His love for Himself as holy. Correspondingly, the divine or moral law is comprehended in love for God. Moreover, God's will is always directed toward Himself as the end or good. Since the holy Lawgiver is both the giver and the end of the law, there is a fitness and a rightness about the law itself. In describing the law Bellamy introduces an apt phrase which was used later by the Edwardeans. He says that law is a "transcript of God."[4]

The law as such is neither alterable nor arbitrary. All mankind, both elect and non-elect, will be subject to it forever. Because of the Antinomian tendency in New England, Bellamy stresses the point that Christ's satisfaction of justice does not effect an abatement of the moral law. Christ's death does not indicate that the law is too severe. On the contrary His death testifies that the law is good. His death publicly expresses the law.[5]

Specific commands of the Lawgiver may be arbitrary,

although the divine or moral law is not so. For example, the command to Adam to abstain from eating fruit from the tree in the midst of the garden might have been arbitrary. However, an arbitrary command is as inviolable as the divine law because it is the expressed will of the Lawgiver. His authority is universal and complete, and His will must be respected. The specific nature of a command from God is not a matter of foremost importance. God's authority must be foremost. The duty to obey derives from the fact that it is God who commands. Bellamy assumes that His commands are always right because of the nature of God. However, if a command does not appear to be reasonable, it is man's duty to obey it because it is God's prerogative to demand obedience to His will.[6]

Although a specific command may be arbitrary, God's threatening punishment for disobedience is never arbitrary. Threatening is inherent in any command since a command that does not involve penalty for disobedience is suggested activity. Edwards' view on threatening is followed here: God's moral obligation to punish a sin is not a consequence of the threatening as such. Moral obligation to punish sin inheres in the very nature of the command from the Lawgiver.[7]

Bellamy states his third basic proposition as follows:

> The design of the mediatorial offices and work of the Son of God incarnate, was to do honour to the divine law, and thereby open a way in which God might call, and sinners might come to him, and be received to favour, and entitled to eternal life, consistent with the honour of the divine government.[8]

This proposition takes for granted the universality of sin and condemnation. Bellamy follows Edwards' view on the primal headship of Adam, the fact and nature of original sin, man's natural ability but moral inability respecting the will, and the voluntary character of sin which is always looked upon as an act rather than as a state. Bellamy deviates from the opinion of Edwards as to the meaning of Christ's satisfaction. Edwards explicitly taught that Christ satisfied commutative and distributive justice. There are occasional statements in Edwards' writings in which the language of general justice is employed. Bellamy on the other hand develops his doctrine of the Atonement within the framework of general justice. He definitely rejects the idea of commutative justice,[9] and yet at times his writing highly suggests distributive justice.[10] Despite these occasional suggestions, Bellamy explicitly affirms that he does not wish to espouse the view of distributive justice. He champions the view that Christ satisfied general or public justice. The Mediator is the God-man. By virtue of the dignity of His person, of His authority as the appointed Mediator, and of His obedience to the divine law even unto death, Christ satisfied general or public justice. Accordingly, he advocates General Atonement.[11]

C. General Justice

BELLAMY'S REJECTION OF the view that Christ satisfied distributive justice is most explicit. Edwards A. Park, commonly recognized as a foremost Edwardean, assembled discourses and treatises on the Atonement by Edwardeans in his *The Atonement*. In his introduction to this collection, Park states the point of view held by Bellamy as follows:

> If Christ literally obeyed the law for those whom he died to save; if he literally endured the whole penalty of their

sin, then it would be unjust to require of them a second obedience when one had been fully rendered; and to threaten against them a second punishment when one had been completely borne; then all men for whom he died will be saved. But all men will not be saved. None but the elect will be saved. Then Christ died for the elect only. Thus the doctrine of Limited Atonement is a necessary result from the doctrine that Christ literally satisfied the demands of the law and of distributive justice. But Dr. Bellamy teaches that the doctrine of Limited Atonement is false. He thus undermines the whole theory of Christ's literal punishment, and supererogatory obedience.[12]

It should be observed that Bellamy does not say a great deal about the nature and intensity of Christ's suffering. He does not leave the reader in doubt, however, as to his view that Christ's suffering was great and that it came upon Him in the exercise of His mediatorial office. In fact, by holding that Christ satisfied general justice, it suffices to maintain that His suffering was unfeigned and that it was attendant to His dying. It is not necessary to hold that He endured a specified quantum of suffering. The point to be understood here is that Bellamy stresses the *public display* of God's vindictive justice in the *death* of His Son rather than the precise nature and intensity of Christ's suffering. At this important point Bellamy differs from Edwards who laid special stress upon the sufferings of Christ.

Here is the pivot of Bellamy's doctrine: God acts in the death of His Son in such a manner as to demonstrate to the world His unrelenting intention to punish sin. He acts to protect the majesty of His law and honor of His government. He acts so that a door or way of mercy may be opened consistent with justice in His moral government. Bellamy illustrates this by referring to the case of Zalucus, which is taken from Grotius' *Defensio Fidei Catholicae de Satisfactione Christi*. Grotius' illustration, widely used later on by the Edwardeans, is as follows:

> When Zalucus made a law, that the adulterer should have both his eyes put out as the punishment of his crime; his inclination to punish adultery, according to what he supposed it deserved, induces him, in order to save his son, who had commited adultery, from losing both his eyes, to consent, that one of his own should be put out instead of one of his. And his consenting to this, and its being actually done, instead of arguing that he was not inclined to punish adultery according to its supposed desert, was really the fullest proof of his inclination so to do, that could have been given.[13]

Emphasis upon Christ's vindication of the law and protection of the integrity of God's moral government is the core in Bellamy's doctrine of the Atonement. General Atonement is related to his views of Christ's satisfaction of general justice since he maintains General Atonement is consistent with general justice. However, when Bellamy's view of General Atonement is seen synoptically it will become apparent that his idea of satisfaction cannot be correlated with his idea of General Atonement because "general" becomes subservient to another factor which definitely limits the scope of Christ's Atonement. Before Bellamy's view of General Atonement is considered, three observations should be made which have a direct relation to his view of satisfaction.

D. Three Pertinent Observations

First, we should observe Bellamy's idea of faith. When the Atonement is related to the satisfaction of general justice, faith must connote something different from that which is commensurate with commutative or distributive justice. This is not always the case in Bellamy's writings.

A comprehensive statement of Bellamy's idea of faith must include these primary elements: enlightenment, acquiescence, and duty. Since enlightenment is a matter of divine illumination it effects regeneration. Enlightenment is God's sovereign act of grace. Man has no part in it. No amount of knowledge and ratiocination can produce enlightenment. The unregenerate soul has neither a sense of the correct dimension of evil nor an appreciation of the beauty of holiness. When the soul is renewed by God or when it is flooded by divine light, sin is seen as it really is—an infinite evil—and God is known to be lovable and worthy of disinterested adoration and obedience.

Moreover, the justice of God in condemning sinful mankind is appraised good and just. Christ's death, therefore, is seen by the elect from a different perspective. The justice of the law is made more resplendent by its vindication in His death.[14] Faith assents to the law and in doing so assents to the verdict of the Lawgiver. The verdict of the Lawgiver is death.

Since the bar of God's mercy has been removed by Christ's satisfaction, whereby He can be "just and the justifier of the ungodly," the duty to accept the law is imposed upon the believer. Duty to obey the law is not removed by illuminating grace. Grace enhances the law. Hence faith is not only a holy act or exercise of the will but it is a holy life, for as Bellamy puts it, true religion *consists in a real conformity to the law and in a genuine compliance with the gospel.*[15]

Second, we should observe that Bellamy's idea of satisfaction removes the tension between God's justice and Christ's mercy. Christ's death did not pay a debt to God's honor and thus entitle man to a reward nor did it effect a change in

God's attitude toward man. Christ's satisfaction was an expression of the unvarying disposition in which Christ, the Mediator, fully concurred. Bellamy declares:

> God did not want a heart to do us justice. Nay, God had an heart overflowing with infinite goodness; witness the gift of his Son. And so no mediator was needful to move the divine compassions, much less to prevent his being too severe with us. Yea, a mediator for any such purpose had been an infinite reproach to the deity. A mediator therefore was needful, in order to the salvation of sinners, for no other purpose, but to do honour to the divine law, which we had dishonoured by our sins.[16]

Finally, it is important to observe that Bellamy's scheme is purely objective. The absence of the subjective aspect may be explained by the slight emphasis that he puts on Christ's suffering. It is His obedience unto death that is stressed. The Edwardean theory differs in this respect. In the Edwardean view, the suffering of Christ is put into high relief. His severe suffering is calculated to be a great deterrent.

E. General Atonement

An important facet in Bellamy's view of the Atonement is his declaration that Christ died for the whole world. His satisfaction has universal reference.

Bellamy's adoption of this view is historically important for two reasons. First, it became the view of the Edwardeans. In contradiction to Edward's theory, this is one of the most apparent and at the same time most noteworthy divergences. Second, Bellamy's adoption of General Atonement is of historical interest because Edwards read Bellamy's *True Religion Delineated* and wrote an approving preface for its publication. This anomaly has puzzled historians studying Edwards' precise position during his later years. It is clear that he espoused Limited Atonement in his published writings, as has been shown in Chapter I of this study. It has been pointed out by Edwards A. Park that Edwards did not hold this view exclusively. The evidence that he did not always advocate Limited Atonement is more inferential than explicit.

There is a historical hiatus here. Inasmuch as two centuries have elapsed since Edwards wrote this commendatory preface it is extremely unlikely that further research will yield an unqualified answer. Be that as it may, it would seem that this observed difference is not so material. If it be said simply that Edwards was an exponent of Limited Atonement and Bellamy advocated General Atonement, it would be correct to conclude that their views clash. A deeper analysis of Bellamy's view will show how Edwards might well have commended Bellamy's treatise without relinquishing or seriously jeopardizing his own position.

To reiterate, Bellamy holds that Christ's satisfaction was for the whole world. Furthermore, Bellamy holds—and this must be underscored—that despite God's demonstration of His unrelenting intention to uphold His holy law and despite the revelation of His willingness to forgive and cleanse the sinner upon the condition of faith—facts which the Atonement declares—mankind *without exception* has rejected and will reject God's simple proffer of grace.

Bellamy maintains that by virtue of this General Atonement and *man's universal rejection of it* God can act as sovereign in electing souls without impugning His honor or the majesty of the law.[17] Edwards' stress on God's sovereignty has been noted. Bellamy is equally insistent that God is soverign in originating, conducting, and applying the Atonement.

Since there is universal rejection of God's proffer of grace and consequently universal condemnation, God is not under obligation to save any soul, Bellamy maintains. If He passes by a soul in His election of other souls, that soul passed by has no ground for complaint. God is dealing justly.[18] And inasmuch as God's name and law have been honored and protected by Christ's satisfaction, God is free to use with impunity any method He may choose for reclaiming those whom He elects. He chooses to reclaim them by irresistible grace through divine illumination. Here Bellamy is following Edwards' view. It is extremely significant that Bellamy says God's proffer of grace is universally rejected, because the common grace given man is not potent enough to effect saving faith. Finally, since God foreknew that His proffer of salvation would be universally rejected, the Atonement was not designed for the nonelect.

However cogent Bellamy's arguments may be in favor of General Atonement, the fact remains that only those whom God elects can be forgiven and justified. This view of election would seem to nullify his argument that the Atonement has universal reference. Thus it is correct to say of Bellamy's view, as it has been said of Edwards', that the controlling factor throughout his scheme is the sovereignty of God. This being the case, the difference between Edwards and Bellamy on the matter of Limited or General Atonement would seem to be more verbal than real. In either instance it is the sovereignty of God which is the controlling factor in originating, conducting, and applying the Atonement. This is paramount!

F. Conclusion

It is warrantable to say that Bellamy fails to relate Christ's suffering and death to the predicament of man. According to Bellamy, Christ's suffering and death were not designed to expiate sin, to offer cogent motivation for man's loving God or to effect man's ennoblement by inducing him to refrain from evil and cleave to good. Actually, what Christ did for man was to place him on a new plane of probation and therefore under the reaffirmed law.

A significant question arises. Is this a *bona fide* probation? Unless the proclamation of the gospel carries to the heart of the hearer a live option to accept or reject God's proffer, would it be either good or moral? Bellamy explicitly affirms that God foreknew that mankind without exception would remain rebellious, and he affirms man's impotence to comply with the gospel without God's special and irresistible grace. The implications of this are twofold. It implies that man is so immersed in evil and so inured by it that he cannot be touched and altered by that life and death which Christianity has held up before the world as the perfect manifestation of selfless devotion and self-sacrifice. Correlatively, it implies that there is something lacking in Christ's efficacy dealing with man's predicament. According to Bellamy's scheme, Christ put man under a more serious condemnation. By opening a door of mercy which man could not enter except by God's electing grace, Christ made more severe the judgment of God upon the nonelect.

Chapter 3

THE DOCTRINE OF THE ATONEMENT IN SAMUEL HOPKINS

I. HOPKINS' AFFILIATION WITH EDWARDS AND BELLAMY

SAMUEL HOPKINS WAS born at Waterbury, Connecticut in 1721. Following his graduation from Yale in 1741, he became a pupil of Jonathan Edwards, Sr. and a guest in his home from December, 1741 until March, 1742. During his long ministerial career, he served two Congregational churches, Great-Barrington, Massachusetts (1743-1769) and Newport, Rhode Island (1770-1803). He was an intimate friend of Joseph Bellamy for many years and of Jonathan Edwards, Jr., Smalley, West, and Emmons, foremost Edwardeans. This accounts for his great importance as a *commune vinculum* between Jonathan Edwards, Sr. and his successors.

When Jonathan Edwards, Sr. died in 1758 his widow put into Hopkins' hands all the notes and manuscripts of her deceased husband. Hopkins scrutinized these with considerable interest and devotion. It was he who wrote the first biography of Edwards and prepared some of Edwards' most noteworthy works for publication.[1] That Hopkins was made custodian of Edwards' notes and manuscripts is historically important. Thanks to his love for Edwards and his sympathetic interest in his teacher's doctrines, the world has been enriched by the publication of sermons and treatises which might easily have been lost if they had fallen into less appreciative hands. Park observes:

> Hopkins was better prepared than any other man to interpret the writings of his teacher. He was the companion in whom Edwards confided more than in any other man, and it was Hopkins who first published some of President Edwards' most decisive statements on the Atonement.[2]

That Hopkins was the custodian of this material is important from another standpoint. Edwards continued to instruct his former pupil as the latter endearingly perused this material. Edwards' unpublished notes and manuscripts comprised Hopkins' principal material for research, with the exception of the Bible, for many years. When it is recalled that Hopkins' study-day began at four or five in the morning and ended after the setting of the sun, a practice which he followed with great regularity, it is not to be wondered at that Edwards' influence is discernible in Hopkins' theology.

Reference has been made to Edwards' preface to Bellamy's *True Religion Delineated.* Hopkins, too, read Bellamy's treatise in manuscript and commended it highly. This was in 1750, forty-three years before Hopkins' *System* was published.

Moreover, it is important to emphasize that Bellamy and Hopkins were intimate friends. They discussed Christian doctrines many times during the years prior to the latter's dismissal from Great-Barrington in 1769. They were drawn together by mutual esteem for Edwards and for each other and by a common interest in theological problems.

Bellamy's influence upon Hopkins' doctrine of the Atonement is considerable. Hopkins follows Bellamy in adopting the governmental view and in espousing General Atonement. He remains true to Edwards about Christ's satisfaction through suffering. Thus we have in Hopkins a combination of Edwards' and Bellamy's views on the Atonement. It would seem incorrect to call this a synthesis because of Hopkins' failure to dovetail these respective views at the most vital point. This failure will be pointed out later.

Hopkins combines Edwards' idea of Christ's satisfaction through suffering with Bellamy's ideas of rectoral framework and of General Atonement. It is not maintained that this was a conscious attempt to synthesize these views. It is maintained that Hopkins was influenced by both Edwards and Bellamy and that their influence is marked and at the same time that Hopkins was an independent thinker. That he did not concur wholly in the views of Edwards or Bellamy is a mark of his independence.

To show the affinity of Hopkins with Bellamy it is necessary to speak of the nature of law, of Christ's satisfaction as having primary respect to the law and moral government, and of General Atonement. A discussion of Hopkins' affinity with Edwards will follow. We can then determine to what extent Hopkins' theory is a synthesis of Edwards' and Bellamy's theories.

II. HOPKINS' DOCTRINE

A. Nature and Intent of Law

HOPKINS IS MOST explicit in his statement about the nature and intent of the law. In his major theological writing, *The System of Doctrines, Contained in Divine Revelation, Explained and Defended,* he affirms:

> The law of God points out the duty of man, and requires of him what is perfectly right, and no more, or less. It cannot therefore be altered in the least degree, so as to require more or less without rendering it less perfect and good. It is therefore an *eternal unalterable rule of righteousness,* which cannot be abrogated or altered in the least *iota,* by an infinitely perfect, unchangeable legislator and governor, consistent with his character, his perfect rectitude and righteousness. This law necessarily implies, as essential to it, a sanction or penalty, consisting in evil, or a punishment, which is in exact proportion to the magnitude of the crime of transgressing it; or the desert of the transgressor, which is threatened to be executed on the offender. This penalty which is threatened must be no more, nor less, than the sinner deserves, or the demerit of the crime. The least deviation from this would render the law so far imperfect, and wrong. Every creature under this law is under infinite obligations to obey it without any deviation from it in the least possible instance through the whole of his existence; and every instance of rebellion tends to infinite evil, to break up the divine government, and bring ruin and misery on all the moral world; therefore every transgression of this law, or neglect to obey it,

> deserved infinite evil as the proper punishment of it. Consequently this evil, this punishment, must be the threatened penalty of the law.[3]

This strong assertion is modified on the page following this excerpt by "in the true meaning of it" and "in the true meaning and spirit of it." Hopkins says:

> Divine threatenings are *predications,* declaring what shall be, and what God will do in case of transgression of his law. And it is as inconsistent with truth not to execute his threatening, *in the true meaning of it,* as it is not to accomplish and bring to pass, what he has declared and promised shall take place. This law therefore must be maintained *in the true meaning and spirit of it;* as the grand and only perfect rule of rectoral justice, rectitude, or righteousness.[4]

These two excerpts do not teach the same thing. The first obviously indicates distributive justice. The introduction of "in the true meaning of it" and "in the true meaning and spirit of it" indicates general justice. General justice is Hopkins' view. He refers Christ's satisfaction to the vindication of the law rather than to the expiation of sin, as we shall see later.

Parenthetically, in comparing these two excerpts we note a peculiarity in Hopkins' style. The reader is sometimes misled by unequivocal statements that are later qualified by a phrase or clause. Another example of this peculiarity will be pointed out when his idea of vicarious suffering is examined.

B. Satisfaction Related to General Atonement

WITH RESPECT TO the meaning of Christ's satisfaction, Hopkins writes:

> Man had fallen under the curse of the righteous and perfect law of God. It was inconsistent with rectoral righteousness, and infinite goodness, to set aside, or disregard this law, in favour of rebellious man, so as to pardon and receive him to favour, without paying any regard to the execution of the curse threatened, in any sense of degree. It was of infinite importance that the law and moral government should be maintained, and the curse threatened, properly and fully executed. This put man out of the reach of divine infinite goodness, unless some expedient could be found, some way be devised, in which the law of God might be regarded and maintained, and the penalty of it executed, consistent with pardoning and showing favour to man. This rendered it necessary that God himself, in the second person of the adorable Trinity, should assume human nature into a personal union, so as to form one person, who is both God and man; and that this person should, in the human nature, be made under the law, and support and honour it by obeying the precepts, and suffering the curse of it, in the room and stead of man. In this way only could man be delivered from the curse of the law, and obtain complete redemption, consistent with divine truth, rectoral righteousness, wisdom, and goodness.[5]

Hopkins follows Bellamy in espousing General Atonement. For example he affirms in his *System*:

> The Redeemer has made an atonement sufficient to expiate for sins of the whole world; and, in this sense, has tasted death for every man, has taken away the sin of the world, has given himself a ransom for all, and is the propitiation for the sins of the whole world, so that *whosoever* believeth in him may be saved, and God can now be just, and the justifier of him that believeth in Jesus. Therefore, the gospel is ordered to be preached to the whole world, to all nations, to every human creature: and the offer of salvation by Christ is to be made to every one, with this declaration, that whosoever believeth, is willing to accept of it, shall be delivered from the curses of the law, and have eternal life.[6]

C. Hopkins' Supralapsarianism

IT WOULD SEEM that Hopkins as well as Bellamy succeeds in nullifying the real significance of General Atonement. It is his extreme supralapsarianism that would tend to void it. Attention should be given to this tenet.

Hopkins holds that God's decrees are eternal. God's foreknowledge does not fix His decrees, as Bellamy says. His decrees are the ground of His foreknowledge.[7] Evil in the universe is necessary "for the greatest possible good."[8] "All moral evil is designed by God to answer a good end, and is overruled for the greatest good."[9] "The good which is occasioned by the presence of evil in the universe overbalances the evil."[10] God "orders how much sin there shall be, and effectually restrains and prevents all that which he would not have take place."[11] Evil, which in itself is undesirable, is foreordained "for his own glory and the good of the universe," and God Himself is the efficient or positive cause of all sin.[12]

Hopkins' supralapsarianism applies to election. He declares:

> The doctrine of election imports, that God in his eternal decree, by which he determined all his works, and fixed everything, and every event, that shall take place from eternity, has chosen a certain number of mankind to be redeemed, fixing on every particular person, whom he will save, and giving up the rest to final impenitence, and endless destruction.[13]

These unequivocal declarations about decrees and election remove every scintilla of doubt as to Hopkins' view of God's sovereignty in applying the Atonement. Hopkins is in perfect agreement with Edwards and Bellamy on this point. In this connection Hopkins' vehement objection to the use of "means" or to "unregenerate doings" should be noted. Bellamy urges his unregenerate listeners to use means, such as repentance, prayer and faithful observance of the eternal demands of the Scripture in the hope that God would apply the Atonement to them. Hopkins, on the other hand, holds that the use of means brings an even greater condemnation upon the unregenerate who fail ultimately to receive the blessings of the Atonement. Moreover, regeneration, which is entirely a sovereign act of God, is nothing short of a miracle. Man is not awakened and illumined by the preaching of the Gospel *per se* nor does the Holy Spirit call and invite all who hear the Word. God, as the only active agent, by an act of sovereign grace must renew the soul, which is entirely passive in this matter, before it can discern and appreciate the meaning and intent of the Gospel. The tenet may be illustrated in this way: if the eye itself be blinded no possible candlepower of light can effect its seeing. The eye must be restored. Then it can see. God must repair depraved man's moral eye before His call and invitation to faith can be effectually made. Thus regeneration precedes faith in the order of salvation, and regeneration is conditioned upon sovereign election.[14]

However much Hopkins may insist upon General Atonement, the vital significance of "general" would seem to be voided by his supralapsarianism.

D. Edwards' View of Suffering Followed

ATTENTION WILL NOW be given to Hopkins' agreement with Edwards' view of Christ's suffering. Since man has transgressed the law, he "has incurred the penalty of this law, and fallen under the curse of it."[15] Christ's mission on earth was to remove the curse of the law by bearing its penalty. We should note carefully what Hopkins has to say as to how the curse may be removed. He declares that "this curse cannot be taken off, and man released, until it has its effect, and all the evil implied in it be suffered."[16] Obviously, this is *quid pro quo* language of the strictest sort. On page after page following this declaration no intimation is given that his view is any other than that of precise penal satisfaction. Then, without warning, the reader comes upon a qualifying phrase which interrupts his thought and causes him to question the conclusion already forming in his mind as to Hopkins' doctrine. A reexamination of the context confirms the first impression: Hopkins does a curious and unaccountable thing. First, he describes Christ's suffering and death in terms which clearly teach precise penal satisfaction. Then he modifies this position by presenting a view of equivalence which coincides with Edwards' idea. At the same time that a transition is made in his view of equivalence, Hopkins presents an equation which became pivotal in the Edwardean scheme: that to suffer for sin and for the sinner is the same thing as to answer the demand of the law that the penalty for sin be executed. It is therefore important to observe this transition for it discloses a peculiarity in his treatment of redemption and an unjustifiable equation.

To observe this sudden shift in Hopkins' treatment it will be necessary to give a few excerpts from his *System*. The following are presented by page sequence.

> Sinful men were under the curse of the law; and in order to redeem them, the Redeemer must take their place under the law, and suffer the penalty, bear the curse for them and in their room, which is expressed in plain and unequivocal words in the preceding chapter. "Christ hath redeemed us from the curse of the law, being made a curse for us." By being made a *curse for us,* can be nothing else but suffering the penalty, the curse of the law, under which we were, and which man must have suffered, had not the Redeemer suffered it for him, as he could not be redeemed in any other way, without destroying the law.[17]

A little further on he declares:

> One important and necessary part of the work of the Redeemer of man,[18] was to make atonement for their sins, by suffering in his own person the penalty or curse of the law, under which, by transgression, they had fallen; so that sinners might be pardoned and saved, consistent with the divine law, and without the least respect to that, or in any degree making it void; but so as to establish and honour the law.[19]

Continuing the development of his view Hopkins writes:

> When it is said "Christ died *for our sins,*" the meaning must be that his death is the atonement and propitiation for sin; and that by it he suffered the evil with which sin is threatened in the law, or the penalty and curse of the law; or that which is equivalent.[20]

"Or that which is equivalent," the final clause in the preceding excerpt, marks a transition in Hopkins' treatment of suffering. Heretofore his expressions connote precise penal satisfaction. Henceforth his thought for the most part coincides with Edwards' view of equivalent. Thus Hopkins says that "the Mediator did not suffer precisely the same kind of pain, in all respects, which the sinner suffers when the curse is executed on him";[21] that "the magnitude of the sufferings of Christ . . . does not wholly consist in the quantity or degree of pain he endured, or in the duration or length of time in which he suffered";[22] that by virtue of the dignity and worth of His person "for the Redeemer to suffer as he did, is an infinite evil";[23] that:

> The evil of the sufferings of Christ . . . is equal to, is as great as the evil which is threatened to the transgressors of the law, and as great as the sinner deserves; yea, it is as great as the endless sufferings of all mankind; for that is no more than infinite; therefore Christ by sufferings, paid a price, and made an atonement sufficient to redeem the whole world from the wrath to come: And it is not owing to any want or defect in this, that all are not saved; for it is *boundless.*[24]

And Hopkins further states:

> And that a way might be opened for a reconciliation, and favour to man, consistent with the divine law which cursed

> him, and with the righteousness and wisdom of the Governor of the world, the Son of God took the place of man, was made under the law, and took the curse upon himself; which therefore was inflicted on him without the least mitigation. This is the reason of these dreadful sufferings of this infinitely great and worthy personage.[25]

"Or that which is equivalent" connotes something in addition to what had been said about it. That is, "equivalent" does not refer only to the nature and intensity of Christ's suffering. Rather, "equivalent" refers to the meaning of that suffering. After saying "or that which is equivalent," Hopkins immediately adds:

> To suffer *for sin* and *for the sinner,* is so far to take place of the sinner, as to suffer the evil which he deserves, and which otherwise the sinner must have suffered. Or, which is the same, the sufferings of Christ answer the same end with respect to law, and divine government, that otherwise must be answered by the eternal destruction of the sinner.[26]

Imputation of sin and distributive justice are definitely suggested in the first part of this excerpt. The primary reference is to man and to his predicament. The idea in the latter part of this excerpt is rectoral. General justice is suggested. The primary reference is to law and to its vindication. According to Hopkins the end answered by the eternal destruction of the sinner is the veracity of God's word and the inexorableness of His vindictive justice. Are the veracity of God's word and the inexorableness of His vindictive justice the primary ends answered by Christ's satisfaction of distributive justice? Is not the expiation of sin the primary end answered by distributive justice? The expiation of sin is not the same thing as vindication of the law. Hopkins, however, equates suffering as an expiation with suffering as a vindication of the law.

Bellamy is more consistent at this point. Since the death of Christ has primary respect to the vindication of the law, the public display of His death is made focal. A door or way of mercy was opened when the law was vindicated. Hopkins, on the other hand, stresses the equivalence of Christ's suffering to the deserved suffering of man and holds that the "mighty bar and obstacle in the way of showing any favour to man, and escaping eternal destruction"[27] is wholly removed by Christ's satisfaction through suffering. Obviously, when the bar is removed by an equivalence of suffering it would seem illogical not to relate suffering primarily to the expiation of sin, for the bar in this instance has reference to distributive justice.

It is important to stress that the expiatory efficacy of suffering is clearly taught by Hopkins. For example, he says:

> If the sinner were to suffer the penalty himself, in his own person, and were able to do this and survive his suffering, this would alter his moral character, as he would then have completely compensated for his crime, it being extinguished by his suffering all the evil which it deserves; no more could be required, or justly inflicted upon him. His whole character being considered, his crimes and sufferings, he would stand right in law, and have no need of a pardon, and there would be no grace in not punishing him yet more.[28]

This passage teaches that suffering is the means of expiating sin. It would not be improper to infer from this that Christ's suffering was for the expiation of man's sin, since the penalty threatened in the law is suffering and since the curse of the law is lifted by Christ's suffering the penalty in man's place. Hopkins, however, rejects this view. The infinite evil in Christ's suffering, being equivalent to the infinite evil threatened in the law, is a vindication but not an expiation. This is so because His suffering has respect to law rather than to the sinners' burden of guilt. Although Hopkins holds that Christ's suffering was infinite, he refuses to allow that man's sin was expiated by Christ's suffering.

Hopkins continues:

> The vicarious sufferings of a substitute are quite different and opposite, in this respect, to the sufferings of the sinner, which have been supposed, though really imposible. For, in the case of the vicarious sufferings, the sinner's character remains the same, and he continues as ill-deserving as ever, and must feel so, if his discerning and feeling be according to truth.[29]

It is important to observe that when he says "he continues as ill-deserving as ever," Hopkins means all mankind, both nonelect and elect, who are forgiven and justified. If Christ has assumed the curse, if the penalty for sin has been imputed to Him and if He had offered adequate satisfaction for sin by bearing its infinite evil, then the legal handwriting has been erased. The sinner, by faith, can justly and exultingly consider himself exonerated before the law. Edwards, as we have seen, holds that the elect, by virtue of Christ's satisfaction and merit, have a just claim on God's forgiveness and reward that have been gratuitously promised them. But Hopkins demurs here. Christ has truly suffered for sin. He has endured an infinite evil but the sins of man were not imputed to Him. On what ground then was it just that the vindictive wrath of God be spilled upon Christ? When one comes under the burden of another's sins and voluntarily allows them to be imputed to him, it is conceivable that he may be justly adjudged worthy of suffering. By rejecting the doctrine of imputation and at the same time holding that Christ satisfied divine justice by suffering, Hopkins leaves himself open for an insistent question which he does not explicitly answer.

Whose sins did Christ bear? Certainly not His own, for the sinlessness of Christ is the indispensable quality which conditions His work. Then He must have borne the sins of man. But Hopkins does not say this. The peculiarity of his thought lies here. The passion of Christ is depicted in such a manner as to answer the demands of distributive justice but His passion is related to general justice. It is extremely significant to observe that neither man's moral nor legal status is altered by Christ's satisfaction. We are not moving here in the realm of imputation of sin upon Christ and the nonimputation of guilt upon the believer, as in the Penal view. It is a different realm from that, and the framework is moralism rather than piety. Although no specific passage can be cited from Hopkins' writings to prove it, the implication from all this is clear. Hopkins conceives of Christ as bearing the penalty of sin through infinite suffering but not bearing the sinners' penalty. In other words, Christ bore the sinners' suffering ideologically but not actually. This conclusion seems especially warrantable because Hopkins relates Christ's satisfaction to the law or to the moral government rather than to the sinner's reconciliation—to vindication of the law rather than to expiation of sin. At precisely this point, Hopkins' theory fails to be a synthesis of Bellamy's rectoral idea and Edwards' doctrine of satisfaction through suffering.

The evidence presented is conclusive that Hopkins duplicates Edwards' idea of Christ's satisfaction through suffering. Christ's suffering is primarily spiritual. It is infinite and equivalent by virtue of His dignity as the only-begotten well-beloved Son of God. The evidence is conclusive that Christ's satisfaction has primary reference to the law or to God's moral government. As in Bellamy, Christ's satisfaction vindicates God's law and protects the integrity of His government. If Hopkins had first applied Christ's satisfaction to man's predicament before the law rather than to the law itself—that is to say, if Christ's satisfaction had been primarily related to expiation and forgiveness of sins rather than to vindication of the justness of the law and of man's condemnation—a synthesis of Edwards' and Bellamy's views would have been established in Hopkins' doctrine. It is entirely conceivable that Christ's satisfaction be primarily related to reconciliation without relinquishing the view that His satisfaction affirms the justness of the law and protects the integrity of God's moral government.

E. Redemption Broader Than Atonement

THE WORK OF redemption is broader than the Atonement, according to Hopkins. The Atonement consists exclusively in Christ's suffering and death. It is effected when the curse of the law or the penalty for sin is borne, but mere vindication of the law is insufficient for man's salvation. This is only the negative aspect of the work of redemption. The positive aspect is the obedience of Christ to the law and His faithfulness in discharging the mediatorial mission.[30] Christ's obedience was necessary in order for the elect to receive a reward. Although Hopkins rejects the idea of imputation with respect to Christ's bearing the sinners' actual guilt, he agrees with Edwards in holding that Christ's merit accrues to the elect. Hopkins also adopts Edwards' use of "patron" and "client."

This is not the first time we have found it explained that Atonement is limited to Christ's suffering and death. This view is implicit in Edwards' distinction between satisfaction and merit. It is present in Bellamy's oft-repeated expression "atonement and merit." But most explicitly it is stated by Hopkins:

> The obedience of Christ, though most excellent and meritorious, is not an atonement for the sins of men, or really any part of it. It is impossible that any mere obedience, however excellent and meritorious, should make atonement for the least sin. This can be done by nothing but suffering the penalty of the law, the evil with which transgression is threatened, as has been shown, while attending to the sufferings of Christ.

> Christ did, indeed, obey in suffering, and this was, perhaps, the highest act or instance of his obedience. As a servant he received a command from the Father to lay down his life to make atonement for the sins of men. . . . And it was necessary that his suffering should be voluntary, and so an act of obedience, as far as he was active, in order to his suffering justly, and making any atonement thereby. But though the Redeemer *obeyed in suffering,* and suffered in obeying; and his highest and most meritorious obedience was acted out in his voluntary suffering unto death, and in this greatest instance of his suffering, the Atonement which he made for sin chiefly consisted; yet his obedience and suffering are two perfectly distinct things, and answer different ends; and must be considered so, and the distinction and difference carefully, and with clearness kept up in the mind, in order to have a proper understanding of this very important subject.[31]

In the foregoing passage we note Hopkins' affirmation that Christ's suffering was an obedient suffering and His obedience was a suffering obedience. How this can be the case, and His suffering and obedience be so sharply demarked that only the former constitutes the Atonement, is not clear. Furthermore, if Christ's satisfaction is to be primarily related to the vindication of the law as Hopkins relates that satisfaction, then obedience becomes an indispensable element in the Atonement itself, for Atonement is not effected by suffering *per se*—not even by the suffering involved in dying shamefully. Atonement is effected by obedience unto death. Edwards is more consistent here. He relates Christ's suffering to the satisfaction of distributive justice. If His obedience is the basis of the elect's reward, as Hopkins makes it, it is quite incorrect not to refer His suffering to the expiation of sin. Expiation and justification—that is to say, forgiveness of sin and bestowment of reward—are complements of an equivalent suffering and perfect obedience. Hopkins makes vindication and justification complementary. Justification has respect to both forgiveness and reward. Expiation, a term Hopkins frequently uses, stands devoid of meaning. It does not have any definite relationship to anything actual, since forgiveness is a sovereign act that does not depend upon the expiation of sin.

There is an unbroken silence in Hopkins' writing about any deterring quality to the public sufferings of Christ. It would seem that his emphasis upon suffering would lead him to magnify its effect upon human behaviour. On second thought, we see how consistent Hopkins is in not setting forth this subjective emphasis. Of what avail is an altered external behaviour when the heart or will is corrupt? Moreover, regeneration which renews man is not a product of an impression such as Christ's suffering makes upon the mind. It is not the result of knowledge, even of the knowledge that Christ died for man, nor is it the end product of a diligent use of means. Regeneration is God's arbitrary act. It has an instantaneous and lasting effect upon the soul.[32] The only element of subjectivity in the Atonement appears in the growing appreciation which the elect have of the majesty of God's law and of the love of Christ in removing the curse of the law for them. This means that the subjective influence of the cross is entirely subsequent to regeneration. Prior to one's regeneration the effect of the cross upon a person is of no avail for his salvation, nor is it a means to his regeneration.

It would seem that Hopkins' chief contribution to the Edwardean scheme lies in his combining the distinctive elements in the theories of Edwards and Bellamy. Viewing the theories of Edwards, Bellamy, and Hopkins synoptically, we have observed that the Edwardean theory resembles Hopkins' theory more closely than it does either Edwards' or Bellamy's. The Edwardean scheme is rectoral and Christ's suffering is magnified in it. These are the emphases of Hopkins.

The fact that these close friends—Edwards, Bellamy, and Hopkins—did not agree with each other on all points with respect to the Atonement indicates more than that they were independent thinkers. It indicates that thought on the Atonement was in a state of flux. It is significant that the internal difficulty of the Old New England view was responsible for this fresh inquiry into the meaning of Christ's suffering and death.

The debate on the Atonement in New England will be treated briefly in Chapter V. That debate occurred following the arrival of John Murray from England in 1770. By that time Edwards was dead (1758), Bellamy's *True Religion Delineated* (1750) and *The Nature and Glory of the Gospel* (1762) had been published, and Hopkins had promulgated his views which were to be incorporated into his *System* (begun 1781 and published 1795). It is important to point out these facts because they are valuable in showing that the Edwardean scheme was not a sudden rebuttal to the Universalists. On the contrary, the pattern of their theory had been long in forming, and the chief elements in their view had been publicly stated by their theological progenitors. The Edwardeans cannot be accused of temporizing.

Chapter 4

THE DOCTRINE OF THE ATONEMENT IN STEPHEN WEST

I. WEST'S AFFILIATION WITH HOPKINS AND BELLAMY

STEPHEN WEST WAS born in Tolland, Connecticut on November 2, 1735. After his graduation from Yale College in 1755, he studied theology under Thomas Woodbridge at Hatfield, Massachusetts. He was the military chaplain at Hoosac Fort for a few years prior to accepting a call to Stockbridge, Massachusetts. Succeeding Edwards, who had left Stockbridge to become the president of Princeton College, West served this congregation from 1759 until his death in 1816. It was there that he became acquainted with Hopkins and Bellamy, and it was largely due to Hopkins' influence that West was converted from Arminianism to "New Divinity," the name commonly given to the theology of Edwards, Bellamy, and Hopkins. Edwards A. Park, in commenting on the historical importance of West, says:

> He was the cherished and confidential companion of Bellamy and Hopkins, and through them became thoroughly versed in the peculiarities of their theological instructor. He was also intimate with Dr. Edwards (Jonathan Edwards, Jr.), Dr. Smalley, and Dr. Emmons, and is thus a connective link between these divines and the triumvirate whom they all revered.[1]

West published three treatises: *Essays on Moral Agency, Evidences of the Divinity of the Lord Jesus Collected from the Scripture,* and *Essay on the Scripture Doctrine of Atonement.* His treatise on the Atonement furnishes the most important material for our investigation.[2]

II. WEST'S DOCTRINE

A. God's Self-disclosure

THE CORE OF West's doctrine of the Atonement is the idea that God loves to act like Himself. Key words in West's discussion of Atonement are *manifest, exhibit, display,* and *glass.* Obviously, West does not hold a priority here, for a common element in the generality of theories on the Atonement is that God discloses Himself, His attributes or character, in the suffering and death of Christ. To say that God does not love to act like Himself or to say that God loves to act unlike Himself would undermine the whole structure of theology. This is too obvious for further elaboration. However, the manner in which West develops his fundamental idea is illuminating.

West insists that the primary aim of the Creator in all His

works is to manifest Himself. All phenomena are mirrors that reflect the presence of God and are designed to make visible some distinctive attribute or attributes of His nature. To change the metaphor, the world speaks a language to the intelligent creation.

The moral law is another conveyance of the divine character. This law is a transcript of the divine perfections, and its enforcement is the *sine qua non* of moral government. God, the moral Governor, acted like Himself in giving the law originally. He consistently acts like Himself in the execution of the law for His own glory and the good of His creation.

In executing the law God rewards righteousness and punishes iniquity. Both rewards and punishments are exhibitions of an identical regard for His holiness or for Himelf as holy. Sanctions are indispensable to the nature of law, since the law is a transcript of the divine perfections. Where there is insolent disobedience of the law the Lawgiver has no other alternative than to express His aversion to sin. Failure to express His reaction to sin by punishment would be to act unlike Himself. Punishment, West emphasizes, is a *glass* in which the character of God may be seen. He does not take a ghoulish delight in punishing sinners. He is unlike a petty ruler who when offended inflicts punishment with punitive vengeance. West, like Anselm, holds that God Himself cannot be injured by man's insolence. "Pain and distress," West writes, "have no moral virtue in them; and are of no importance, otherwise than as *means* through which the beauty of the divine character, and the true disposition of the divine mind, may be seen by his creatures."[3] Thus, pain and distress are expressions of the divine recoil against evil. The seat of suffering is in the mind. Suffering is the evidence of God's haunting, inescapable presence expressing abhorrence against man's sin, for West continues, "the righteousness of the law is fulfilled in the *sufferings of the sinner,* in no other way than as they serve to exhibit the righteous character of God, and prove him to be a hater of iniquity."[4]

B. Atonement, A Reflecting Glass

THE ATONEMENT IS a *glass* reflecting divine abhorrence and indignation against the sinner. We should pause here to emphasize West's idea that the design of the Atonement is to exhibit the attributes of God to man. If God forgave any person without making vivid His abject abhorrence of evil, His real disposition towards the sinner would be misapprehended. It would be fatal to the fellowship between God and man if the sinner failed to appraise properly God's holy abhorrence against evil. Moreover, it is in the poignant awareness of God's displeasure against the sinner that the radiance of His grace is seen. If His abhorrence of sin fails of expression, the freeness of His grace will not be appreciated. Grace is offered at a frightful cost to God, since sin is abjectly abhorred by Him. Thus, if God's abhorrence of sin were not displayed to the sinner, the fear of sinning—not the fear of punishment *per se*—would not be impressed upon man's heart. God's true disposition toward sin is the only potent deterrent to sin and it is also the only motivation to obedience. It is God's nature that both deters man from sinning and induces his obedience. West, as a true disciple of Edwards, rejects the idea that fear of punishment and hope of reward are pure motives. Disinterested benevolence—virtue that makes God Himself the chief end—finds its motivation in the nature of God as holy.

The Atonement exhibits the same attributes of God that would have been displayed in the eternal punishment of sinners. As West explains, "For eternal torments inflicted on sinners by the great Governor of the world, express nothing in action, but what the threatenings of the law express in words."[5] Punishment, as has been observed, signifies divine aversion to sin and serves to give a "clear and sensible manifestation of His divine displeasure against the sinner."

This explanation of punishment is the hinge on which West's doctrine turns. The central stress is upon God's abhorrence of evil and is most clearly manifested in punishment. Atonement is contingent upon the possibility of God's full exhibition of His abhorrence in a manner other than that of exacting the full need of suffering from the sinner. One may ask: is there a way by which the sinner can be relieved of his suffering the just punishment for his demerits, and is there a way by which God's displeasure against the sinner can be exhibited and His broken law honored? West replies that Christ's suffering and death answer affirmatively this twofold inquiry. He states his view of the Atonement as follows: "that which magnifies the broken law of God, and does it the same honor, which would have been done by the execution of its penalty whenever it be incurred."[6]

C. Christ's Suffering and His Obedience

We have observed that the law is a transcript of the divine perfections; that punishment is an exhibition of the divine aversion to sin; and that Atonement is effected whenever the divine abhorrence is fully expressed and, at the same time, the way of salvation opened for the return of the sinner to God. Since the Atonement was effected by the mediatorial work of Christ we want to know what West has to say regarding the nature and intensity of Christ's suffering and of His obedience.

West writes that "the *sacrifice and sufferings of Christ* were a lively demonstration of the righteous displeasure of God against sinners."[7] With apparent ardor he declares:

> That Christ should *himself* become the price of the sinner's redemption—that he should give *himself, his life,* a ransom for sinners—that he should be *made sin, suffer, die, and be sacrificed for them;* are expressions which convey a sense too plain and intelligible to be easily evaded. And, if these and such like expressions, do not imply that, for some reason or other, Christ verily *substituted himself and subjected himself to suffering and death, in the room* and place of sinners; it will be difficult to find language, to invent terms, which would fully and unequivocally ascertain *this* idea of the end of his death.[8]

However, these affirmations of vicariousness still leave us in doubt about West's precise ideas of imputation of sin to Christ and of equivalence of His suffering to the suffering deserved by man. With respect to equivalence, it is clear that West did not teach that the suffering of Christ was the same kind and the precise amount as the law threatens. Nevertheless, by virtue of His dignity, Christ's suffering was infinite and therefore equivalent. He follows Edwards in laying stress upon the spiritual nature of Christ's suffering, maintaining that God conveyed to the mind of Christ a dreadful sense of the divine abhorrence of sin. This was especially true with respect to the frightful suffering of Christ in Gethsemane and on the cross.

Although West's view of imputation has affinity with the view Edwards himself espoused, the Edwardeans, Edwards' successors, opposed it. It would not be far from the truth to say that West's doctrine of imputation is a throwback to the Penal Doctrine. He explicitly affirms that the evidence from Scripture supports the view "that the crimes of men are expiated by the sufferings of Christ."[9] He states: "The sword of God, the sword of divine justice, was called up, and commissioned against Christ and smote, and took away his life."[10]

West's use of interchange is extremely significant, if it is to be taken at face value.

> To see the fruits of divine anger alight upon the immaculate Lamb of God, when he came to deliver his people from the power of sin, and from the wrath and curse of God, and, then, behold the people of Christ, who are themselves infinitely guilty, reaping the happy fruits of divine righteousness; so strongly indicates, in itself, an interchange of persons, between Christ and his people, as to sufferings and rewards, as hardly leaves room for a doubt whether this were really the case.[11]

Because of the extreme importance of this point both in determining West's view of imputation and in ascertaining its affinity with the Edwardean theory, one more significant aspect of his treatment of imputation should be presented.

West argues that displeasure against the guilty is expressed by sufferings brought on the innocent. He maintains both the necessity of the innocent suffering for the guilty and the possibility that God's displeasure against the guilty can be expressed by suffering brought on the innocent.

> To say, therefore, that displeasure against the *guilty,* cannot be expressed by evils brought on an *innocent person,* at once denies, either the necessity of punishment; or room for pardon. For if it be essential to the glory of God, that he express displeasure against wickedness *by any natural evils;* these evils must be endured, either by the *guilty,* or by some one who is *innocent.* If they are en-

> dured, by the wicked themselves, the sinner *is not,* yea, cannot be pardoned. If the sinner be pardoned, and the displeasure of God nevertheless expressed in *natural evils;* it must of necessity be that this is done in natural evils brought on one who is *innocent.*[12]

It is imperative that West's connotation of *display* be understood in order to avoid any misinterpretation of his view about Christ's suffering on the Atonement. A display may be a mere representation of the real. It may be an ostentatious parade devoid of reality. It may be something feigned merely to impress spectators. West does not mean any of these. Display is the external complement of an internal reality. It is a visible and overt counterpart of an invisible and otherwise occult experience. In the Christian experience of forgiveness, the reality of Christ's vicarious sacrifice becomes vivid. Christ's suffering and death in the room of man were not a mere display. They were the display of the reality of His sacrifice in lieu of man's eternal death. West's basic principle is that God loves to act like Himself. He affirms that God's aversion to sin is unvarying. If the sufferings and death of Christ were a mere display or if the sins of man were not imputed to Him then God would be acting unlike Himself in the Atonement. That is to say, God would be giving an impression of His character through the medium of Christ's feigned suffering, or He would be exhibiting His aversion to sin where there was no real or imputed sin. Thus, the passion of Christ would become a simulation. But for West it was not a simulation nor was Christ's suffering a display of God's wrath against Christ. The display was an exhibition of God's righteous judgment against man. Park significantly observes:

> Dr. West often repeats the remark that, as all the ills of life are expressive of God's anger, so the natural evils which Christ endured express the same; but this accurate writer is peculiarly careful to add, that this anger is against *sinners*. 'If, in the sufferings and death of Christ, God expressed any degree of anger, whatever, it must have been *against sinners;* because no degree of it existed against Christ.' It need not be said that there is no literal penalty of the law which does not express the anger, or rather the distributive justice of the lawgiver against the person punished.[13]

According to West, Christ's obedience is not a part of the Atonement. His suffering and death constitute the Atonement—especially His death. It was by His dying that the divine abhorrence of evil was exhibited. Christ's obedience answers one grand and indispensable end; it is that conditioning quality that rendered His suffering and death acceptable to the Father.

D. Satisfaction Applied to General Justice

THE APPLICATION OF Christ's suffering to the satisfaction of general justice in West's scheme would seem to be indefensible. If Christ suffered excruciatingly in man's room and if the sin of man were imputed to Christ as West affirms, it would seem irregular to relate this primarily to general justice. To satisfy general justice it is not requisite that the sanction of the law be precisely fulfilled. This is especially true when it is affirmed that Christ's suffering was incalculably enhanced by virtue of the dignity of His person and when it is affirmed that His suffering was primarily a poignant awareness of the holy aversion of God to the sins of man. These are explicit tenets in West's doctrine. The literal penalty of the law cannot be more excessive than infinite suffering, the degree of suffering Christ endured. Imputation cannot be expressed in a more precise term than interchange. "Infinite suffering" and "interchange" speak the language of distributive justice. Therefore it would seem that West's idea of Christ's suffering and his idea of imputation do not correlate with general justice.

Also, by the same token, West seems to err in making exhibition the central matter in the Atonement. If an exhibition reveals that which is real, the material thing is primary. West's idea of exhibition is nothing short of a manifestation of the expiation of sin. We have observed that his use of *exhibit* or *display* connotes a conveyance of something real or substantial. The cross is visual language. If Christ's sufferings were infinite by reason of the gravity of sin which He bore and by reason of the dignity of His person then it must be said that what He exhibited was the divine abhorrence of sin in the act of expiating it. The material aspect, therefore, is the expiation of sin. The exhibition is a factor attendant to the material aspect. This puts us back into the framework of the Penal theory according to which the holy indignation of God is evidenced in Christ's expiatory sacrifice.

Furthermore, if Christ bore the penalty of imputed sin as West construed *impute* and *penalty,* can it be said that there was a genuine relaxation of the sanction of the law? The threatening cannot be more severe than an infinite evil. Christ's suffering was infinite. It answers the same end as the eternal damnation of sinners would have answered. Therefore, the principle of relaxation is of no great moment in this scheme.

E. Some Insistent Questions

WEST'S THEORY POSES a number of insistent questions. First, there are questions arising out of his emphasis upon a display of God's aversion to sin, an emphasis which tends to vitiate God's display of mercy. Is it not just as important that Christ's death be set forth as a display of divine mercy as of divine judgment? Does it not follow from advocating imputation of sin that Christ's death is as much a display of mercy as of abhorrence against sinners? Is it imperative that God display His aversion to sin rather than His boundless love before mercy be safely offered? If God may relax the precise sanctions of the law out of regard to Christ's display of divine abhorrence, may not the law be relaxed out of regard for a display of God's mercy? Assuming, as does West, that disinterested obedience is true virtue, is God's display of aversion to sin the highest divine impulse to man's disinterested obedience?

Second, there are insistent questions growing out of West's contention that appreciation of mercy is deepened by the elect's awareness of the judgment of God upon the nonelect and growing out of the contention that moral evil is ultimately a universal good. Is it necessary to an appreciation of a *good* that the beneficiary of it be aware of an evil in another's life? Does a heightened sense of mercy derive from a knowledge of and display of God's condign punishment upon others? Would the prodigal Son's joy, for example, have been enhanced by his father's disinheritance of the other brother?

Third, there are questions growing out of the entire governmental concept. Does this scheme coincide with Christ's idea of the Fatherhood of God? Does the governmental concept set forth adequately the personal relation of

God and man? Does God rule the world with general good in view, or does He rule the world with individuals in view with whom He deals as sons?

We have observed that both Bellamy and Hopkins make focal Christ's vindication of the law. West does not deny that this may be a by-product of Atonement, but he refuses to make it the chief end. He insists that the elect alone will see a vindication of the law in Christ's death. The nonelect cannot see in His death a vindication of the law.

It is anomalous, at least, that West bases the subjective value of the Atonement on the very principle that he attacks with respect to vindication. According to West, the presence of natural evils, including physical death, is the exhibition of God's displeasure against man. Physical death with its involvement of suffering came by sin. Everyone witnesses this phenomenon in the world. If a person does not see an exhibition of God's abhorrence of man's iniquity in this constantly recurring phenomenon, how can he see an unmistakable display of God's displeasure against sin in Christ's suffering and death? Apart from faith, does anyone see in the external doings surrounding Christ's death evidence that His suffering was greater than that which was ever borne by another condemned person? Apart from one's appraisal of Christ's sinlessness, can he see in the Saviour's suffering the hand of God at work laying the penalty of man's sin upon Christ? It is faith which sees His death as an Atonement and faith is not evoked by the mere knowledge that once upon a time a person was crucified on a cross. Faith is evoked by the combination of fact, interpretation of fact and an offer of that which the fact indicates; namely, by the knowledge that what was done was done for me and that its benefits are now being offered to me. Faith in Christ, however faith may be defined, must first find exceeding worth in Him before it discovers exceeding worth in what He did upon a tree.

Thus, by employing the very psychological principle West used to attack the idea of vindication, we may attack the subjective value that West puts upon the display of God's abhorrence of evil in Christ's death. Furthermore, the subjective element in West's view is limited by an important factor to which our attention will now be drawn

F. God's Sovereignty in Redemption

West clearly favors the doctrine of General Atonement. He declares that a "foundation is laid, sufficiently broad, for the general invitations of the gospel; and for the joyful proclamation, that whoever will, may come and take of the waters of life freely."[14] This is excellent material for the pulpit and good news for the congregation. But what is said cannot be taken at par value! That is to say, broad is the invitation to the waters of life but sovereign election has so ordered it that few be those who drink.

West agrees with Edwards, Bellamy, and Hopkins in holding that God is sovereign in conducting and applying the Atonement. However much these writers differ with respect to the precise nature and intention of Christ's mediatorial mission, they are at one in affirming sovereign election. It is this doctrine, more than any other, that unites them with each other and with the exponents of the Edwardean theory.

Chapter 5

THE EDWARDEAN DOCTRINE OF THE ATONEMENT

I. THE DEBATE ON THE ATONEMENT

THE EFFECTUAL PROPAGATION of Universalism in New England during the latter part of the eighteenth century evoked debate on the Atonement.[1] The primary occasion for the debate was the preaching of John Murray, a native of England, who came to Massachusetts in 1770. He was a convert of Whitefield but later became a follower of James Relly.[2]

Foster states that Relly had propounded the doctrine of universal salvation in its extremest form in a book entitled *Union; or A Treatise of the Consanguinity and Affinity between Christ and His Church.*[3] In this treatise Relly maintains that the natural and moral union between Adam and his posterity is an analogue of the spiritual union between Christ and all mankind. This spiritual union is so inextricable that it may properly be called an identification. Thus, the sins of man become Christ's sins and His righteousness becomes man's righteousness. Since Christ has united Himself with man the benefits of His suffering and death accrue to the favor of everyone. No one will be ultimately lost.[4]

Murray supported Relly in this view. The effect of Murray's preaching was rapid and widespread. A congregation was founded at Gloucester, Massachusetts about 1779, and other congregations quickly sprang up as a result of the enthusiastic promulgation of Universalism.

Included among the considerable number of early converts to Universalism was Charles Chauncy, who had earlier attacked the Whitefieldian revival methods. He published a number of excerpts from the writings of foreign Universalists. A tract entitled "Salvation for All Men Illustrated and Vindicated as a Scripture Doctrine" was anonymously published in 1782. The following year another tract appeared anonymously. It was later disclosed that both writings were from the hand of Chauncy. Later he published other treatises in which he vigorously advocated Universalism. His efforts were supported by Hosea Ballou, II, whose influence in establishing Universalism in New England was very effective.[5]

Both New England Calvinists and followers of Jonathan Edwards, Sr. (hereafter referred to as President Edwards) attacked the position taken by the Universalists. Among the Calvinists who opposed Universalism were Samuel Mather, Joseph Eckley, Peter Thacher, and George Beckwith. Among the successors of President Edwards, noteworthy opponents of Universalism were Hopkins, Nathanael Emmons, and Jonathan Edwards, Jr. (hereafter referred to as Doctor Edwards).

Universalism, according to Relly and his followers, rests upon a specific interpretation of Christ's sacrifice. The significant fact is that the Universalists espouse the Penal theory which had been generally held in New England. The Universalists contended that since Christ has borne the penalty for sin both qualitatively and quantitatively, the justice of God has been completely satisfied and all mankind has been redeemed. The New England Calvinists agreed with the Universalists about Christ's punitive suffering, but they maintained that only the elect would be saved. Thus, the debate on the Atonement between Calvinists and Universalists resolved itself into a polemic concerning election rather than an argument about the nature of Christ's satisfaction. The successors of President Edwards, on the other hand, debated the question concerning the nature of the Atonement itself.

The teachings of the Universalists evoked the systematization of a theory of the Atonement which was novel in New England. That theory is now known as the Edwardean theory. It first appeared in three sermons which were delivered in 1785 at New Haven by Doctor Edwards. Williston Walker observes in *A History of the Congregational Churches in the United States*:

> This new Edwardean theory did not indeed spring from the exigencies which brought it out. Its principles lie back in the teachings of the elder Edwards and his contemporaries, though the full meaning of those principles was not perceived by them.[6]

Within six months after Doctor Edwards presented the full-fledged Edwardean theory, John Smalley advocated the same view in his celebrated Wallingford sermons on "Justification through Christ, an Act of Free Grace" and "None but Believers Saved through the All-Sufficient Satisfaction of Christ."[7] The theory gained favor rapidly and soon became the dominant thought on the Atonement in New England. It remained the prevailing view there for more than a hundred years. Among the leading exponents of this view, in addition to Doctor Edwards and Smalley, were Jonathan

Maxcy, Nathanael Emmons, Edward D. Griffin, Caleb Burge, William R. Weeks, Edwards A. Park, and Timothy Dwight.[8]

In scrutinizing the Edwardean theory we should keep in mind two important questions. First, what answer did the Edwardeans give to the Universalists? Second, what novel elements are discoverable in the full-fledged Edwardean theory that did not appear in the writings of President Edwards, Bellamy, Hopkins, and West?

It should be noted here that these Edwardeans do not follow a single pattern in developing their sermons and essays on the Atonement and that their opinions on all related questions do not coincide. They were independent thinkers. Their published writings were prepared with different purposes in view. However, they are in perfect accord with respect to the four major elements in the Edwardean theory: (1) law and its sanctions (2) the necessity for the Atonement (3) the nature of the Atonement and (4) the extent of the Atonement. These four elements will constitute the topics for our present investigation.

II. LAW AND ITS SANCTIONS

THE EDWARDEANS FASHIONED their doctrine of the Atonement according to the relations between a good monarch and his subjects. The framework for their theory may be stated in the following analogical manner: A government cannot long endure if it does not have a law definitive of the duties and prohibitions of its citizens and if the government with its regulatory laws is not respected. So that the law be effective it must be just in itself and it must be adjudged to be just by those who are subject to it. The law must be invariably enforced, else the good name of the state will be sullied and disrespect for the law will ensue.

Invocation of the penalty against any offender enhances regard for the law and deters would-be offenders. On the other hand, respect for the law results in the good estate of the citizens. Not only does the governor of the land praise and reward the people for their good behaviour, but the people develop a spirit of mutual esteem and cooperation as a consequence of their common respect for the law and the government which the law represents and supports.

The Edwardeans maintained that God is the Governor. He has revealed a just law by which He rules. He enforces it for the highest good of the government. Since He rules by law and the subjects' response to His rulership is motivated by reward and punishment, His is a moral government. Inasmuch as an offense is not against the person of the Governor, His punishment of the guilty does not express personal vindictiveness. The Edwardean theory of the Atonement must be seen from this perspective.

It should be observed that the law is not an artifice to keep those subject to it under control. It is not an arbitrary rule imposed upon man. It is a transcript of the divine perfections. As such the law is a rule which coincides with the nature of God and with the ultimate nature of moral relationships among intelligent creatures. This view of law stems from President Edwards, and it finds support in Bellamy, Hopkins, and West.

The divine law is good because it is the language of God's love. His intention in giving and executing it is His own glory and the highest good of man. The fact that law is grounded in the character of God cannot be too strongly emphasized nor can it be too strongly emphasized that the Edwardeans make love the all-controlling attribute of God. What Emmons says in his discourse, "The Purchase of Christ's Blood," is a direct derivative from President Edwards' view and is representative of all Edwardeans.

> God is love. Before the foundation of the world, there was no ground for considering love as divided into various and distinct attributes. But after the creation, new relations arose; and in consequence of new relations, more obligations were formed, both on the side of the Creator and on that of his creatures. Before created beings existed, God's love was exercised wholly towards himself. But after moral beings were brought into existence, it was right in the nature of things that he should exercise right affections towards them, according to their moral characters. Hence the goodness, and the justice, and the mercy of God are founded in the nature of things. That is, so long as God remains the Creator, and men remain his creatures, he is morally obliged to exercise these different and distinct feelings towards them. He must be disposed to do good to the innocent, to punish the guilty, and at the same time to forgive them.[9]

The Edwardeans definitely grounded law in God's character. By insisting upon this presupposition the Edwardeans rejected voluntarism, a characteristic element in New England Calvinism. They were reflecting President Edwards' emphasis upon holiness-benevolence.

Since the law is grounded in the character of God, who is love, it makes its demand with the highest good of the universe in view, as well as to the glory of God Himself. The Edwardeans are careful to point out that whether the law becomes effective by rewarding the obedient or by punishing the disobedient it is the same highest good that induces the Governor to act. Park, in *Discourses on some Theological Doctrines as Related to the Religious Character,* expresses this Edwardean idea in the following manner:

> Our benevolent Father does not administer his moral

> government under the influence of a limited attribute alone; not under the influence of mercy or grace or distributive justice without any regard to the general welfare; not under the influence of a choice of the general without any regard to the demands of distributive justice or the pleadings of mercy or grace; but he administers his moral government under the influence of a general attribute looking at sin and at pardon in all their relations, and providing for the greatest and highest welfare of the universe. Under the influence of this general attribute our benevolent Father resists the plea of mercy and of grace when the safety of the universe requires him to resist it; he yields to the demand of distributive justice when the general good requires him to comply with it; his distributive justice holds the scales and his general justice holds the sword; the former urges its claims and the latter complies with them on the ground of their rectitude and on the condition of their necessity for the general welfare.[10]

Sanctions are necessary for law. They must be invoked whenever the law is broken because the government is thereby protected. Otherwise, "the law of God, which is as near to him as his own nature, would be universally violated and condemned."[11] Park further affirms:

> Penalties he must threaten in order to arrest the in-roads of sin, for sin is ruin; and what he threatens he must inflict, for he is veracious, and his infliction will secure the tempted from the guilt into which they would otherwise plunge. . . . If a single edict would be repealed, or a single penalty mitigated, he foresees the havoc which would ensue, and his kindness forbids the abrogation of a single iota of his commands.[12]

Eternal death is the threatened penalty for sin. It must be kept in mind that the Edwardeans conceive of sin as infraction of the law. They do not conceive of it as personal injury to God. Thus, in punishing man God is not redressing a personal grievance. He is acting as the moral governor for the good of His dominion. Smalley affirms in "The Law in all Respects Satisfied by our Saviour, in Regard to Those only Who Belong to Him; or, None but Believers Saved through the All-Sufficient Satisfaction of Christ" that:

> God delighteth not in the death of the wicked. The misery of his creatures, however justly merited, cannot be an ultimate object of a being whose name, and whose nature is love. The end of the awful threatening and curse of the law, we are to suppose, was discountenancing disobedience, and giving an eternal manifestation of the glorious character of God, as one who infinitely hateth all iniquity.[13]

We should mark here a distinction between Grotius' theory and that of the Edwardeans. Hugh A. Foster says in *A Genetic History of New England*:

> As presented by Grotius, the theory was legal in its forms and without the ideal side. That ideal was given by the Edwardean theory of virtue. God's government rests upon his character, and that character is love. Love puts men under a moral government, and controls them from motives.[14]

Since the law is a transcript of God, grounded in His immutable nature, it is unalterable. According to Grotius, positive law is grounded in the will of God. Being subject to His will, the law can be relaxed if He sees fit to do so.

It has been relaxed in favor of man on account of Christ's passion, Grotius maintains. This is a different point of view from that of the Edwardeans. According to them, law inheres in the very nature of God. Therefore the law is inflexible. Christ's satisfaction neither alters the demands and threatenings of the law nor does it alter man's status before it.

Nevertheless the principle of relaxation is indispensable to the Edwardean scheme. However, it is applied differently. It should be underscored that Grotius applied the principle to the law itself; the Edwardeans to the penalty of the law. According to the latter the law cannot be relaxed, for it is grounded in the very nature of God. But the threatened penalty of the law may be relaxed. It was pointed out in Chapter I that President Edwards held that the threatening of the law was not consequent upon the threatening *as a threatening*. Therefore it is just as inviolable as the law itself. The Edwardeans do not follow President Edwards on this score. Their theory turns on the principle that the punishment threatened in the law can be relaxed when the purpose for which the threatenings are given is satisfied. Griffin declares in "An Humble Attempt to Reconcile the Differences of Christians Respecting the Extent of the Atonement" that:

> The legal threatening is not a pledge of truth that the sinner will be punished: (for then how is that pledge redeemed when he is pardoned by the sufferings of another?) but a mere declaration of what is just, and may ordinarily be expected.[15]

The view of the Edwardeans on law and its sanctions agrees for the most part with that of President Edwards. Law is grounded in the nature of God. The demands it makes upon man derive from Him who gave it. Its effectual operation is an expression of the attributes of God. The all-controlling attribute is love.

The Edwardeans do not accept President Edwards' view that the threatening of the law is as inviolable as the law itself. They hold that its sanctions can be relaxed, if the purpose for which the sanctions were ordained is fulfilled. Since the penalty could be relaxed, it was not indispensable that Christ suffer the precise punishment the law threatened.

III. THE NECESSITY OF THE ATONEMENT

The necessity of the Atonement presupposes the universality of sin. However, the Edwardeans do not hold that the sin of Adam is imputed to his posterity. Every man makes Adam's sin his own by a voluntary act of disobedience. The fact that Adam sinned is the ground for the certainty that every discrete person will sin, although there is no absolute inherent necessity that he do so. George Fisher observes in *History of Christian Doctrine*:

> Hopkins brought in the doctrine of "divine efficiency" in the production even of sinful choices. This is deduced from Edwards' doctrine of a prior infallible certainty of their recurrence. From this time, imputation is discarded from the New England theology. The theory of the Covenant, with Adam as a representative, is exchanged for the theory of "sovereign constitution," or fixed, established connection. Thenceforward the doctrine was that Adam's sin carried with it, by a divine decree, the certainty of his descendants being sinners from the outset of their personal being.[16]

Inasmuch as the threatened penalty for sin is eternal death, the universality of sin signifies that every soul is under sentence of death. This frightful status of man before the law cannot be altered by anything that he can do. In fact he does not will to do anything about it. He wills neither to repent nor to obey, and he will do neither unless induced by God to do so. The disinclination of man must first be broken. He can obey if he wills to do so but he does not so will. His natural ability was not impaired by the fall nor by his own sin. His moral ability has suffered loss. It is important to point out that the whole structure of the Edwardean concept of government and consequently of the Atonement rests upon the presupposition of man's natural ability. Regarding the moral state of man, Maxcy's affirmation in "A Discourse Designed to Explain the Doctrine of the Atonement" is pertinent. He says:

> It is a state of entire alienation of affection from God. That is, it is a state in which the moral temper is averse to divine and spiritual things, insensible of their excellency, and regardless of their importance. . . . Man's depravity does not imply that he is destitute of all the natural ability on which the propriety of the divine commands and injunction rests. If he be not a moral agent, if he have not ability to obey, it does not appear that he can be capable of disobedience. Deity will never censure a blind man for not seeing, nor an idiot for not being wise. He requires the exercise of nothing further than the capacity he bestows. All the depravity of man consists in the wrong use of his natural powers, and in his unwillingness to use them as God requires.[17]

Assuming that man wills to repent and does repent, that act would be insufficient ground for his salvation. God is the moral governor who rules according to law for the highest good of His government. If He forgave without an Atonement, His true disposition toward sin would not be manifest. In urging the inadequacy of mere repentance, the Edwardeans were attacking the Socinians who held that sin was the only bar to man's salvation and that Christ came to evoke man's repentance. Doctor Edwards and Burge lift their theological cudgels against the New England Socinians. Doctor Edwards, in his treatise on "The Necessity of the Atonement," declares:

> The dilemma is this:—eternal justice either requires that every penitent be pardoned in consequence of his repentance merely, or it does not. If it do require this, it follows, that pardon is an act of justice and not of grace; therefore let the Socinians be forever silent on this head.[18]

Parenthetically, substituting "grace" for "justice" and "justice" for "grace," one may use the expression of Doctor Edwards to rebut his argument. One may say: "Either grace requires that every penitent be pardoned in consequence of his repentance merely, or it does not. If it does require this, it follows that pardon is an act of grace and not of justice." After all, repentance has respect to grace and not to justice. The salvation of the elect is entirely a matter of grace and not of justice, as Doctor Edwards himself holds, but the Atonement has absolutely nothing to do with making God's grace effectual in an individual's life! The Atonement was effected not for us as persons but for the government of God.

Burge's answer to the Socinians follows different lines. He explicitly states an Edwardean opinion which has been referred to already in this chapter. He says that sin is "an offence against God, in a public capacity, as the Supreme Governor of the universe." He goes on to explain in "An

Essay on the Scripture Doctrine of Atonement, Showing its Nature, its Necessity, and its Extent" that:

> For, if sin be injurious to God in a private personal capacity only, and he be not an inexorable but a compassionate being, he might certainly pardon, at least as many sinners as repent, without any atonement whatever. But sin should not be considered in this light. It is an offence against God, in a public capacity, as the Supreme Governor of the universe. Hence, notwithstanding God is infinite in benevolence and compassion, he cannot grant pardon to sinners, unless it can be done under such circumstances, and in such a way, as render it consistent with the highest interest of the great community over which his government extends.[19]

The point is this. If it were a strictly private and personal relationship between God and an individual there would be no reason for God to withhold forgiveness from the repentant. Neither commutative nor distributive justice would have to be satisfied as a prerequisite to forgiveness. The Edwardeans strongly affirm that God, as the governor of the universe, deals corporately with persons for the general good of His government. It is on this basis that repentance is insufficient, and Atonement is necessary.

That the Atonement is necessary entirely on God's account is the central and common emphasis of all exponents of the Edwardean theory. It should be stated clearly at this point that "on God's account" does not mean that the Atonement does something *to* Him or that the Atonement causes Him to be merciful or benevolent. "On God's account" means that God does something for Himself. All theories of the Atonement presuppose that God initiates redemption. However, there is something unique in the Edwardean view. The Commercial and Penal theories suppose that something must be done—either a debt must be paid or a quantum of punishment must be endured—before God's mercy can become effective in forgiving those who repent. The barrier to mercy in these instances is the justice of God. The Edwardean approach is different. It is not necessary for something to be done *to* God, for the *locus* of the barrier to mercy is not *in* God.

The view of the Edwardeans is seen in what they disavow as well as in what they affirm. Therefore, attention will be given to certain ideas which they reject as well as to the view they hold.

It is important to stress that according to the Edwardeans the Atonement was not effected in order to make God benevolent or compassionate. It has not enhanced to the least degree His kind disposition toward man. In his "Essay on the Atonement" to which we have already referred, Burge declares:

> Some have supposed it was necessary to conciliate the divine feelings, and render God propitious. They have imagined, that when man sinned, the anger of God was so enkindled against him, and his indignation so excited, as to exclude from his bosom all compassion towards him, and all disposition to do him good; and hence that the Atonement was necessary to cool the divine anger, and to produce in the mind of God, a disposition more favorable to the sinner. . . . If there had been no atonement, his compassion would have been the same. If atonement had been impossible, or in the view of infinite wisdom, ineligible, still the divine compassion would have been just as great, as it is now since Christ has died. . . . For surely, if God had not been benevolent, if he had not been gracious, and full of compassion to sinners, he would

> never have concerted the scheme of atonement, at infinite expense, to do them good.[20]

The Atonement was not necessary to satisfy distributive justice. Smalley indicates for us the Edwardean attitude on this point in his reply to the Universalists. Incidentally, the Edwardean position about the necessity and the nature of the Atonement was a direct rejection of the views espoused by the Universalists. Smalley declares in "None but Believers Saved through the All-Sufficient Satisfaction of Christ" that:

> The argument stands thus. God is obliged in justice to save man as far as the merit of Christ extends: but the merit of Christ is sufficient for the salvation of all man; therefore God is obliged in justice to save all. The minor proposition I dare not deny. I question not the sufficiency of the merit of Christ for the salvation of all mankind. I have no doubt but that, in this sense, Christ "gave himself a ransom for all; tasted death for every man; and is the propitiation for the sins of the whole world." The only thing therefore which I have to dispute in this argument, is the obligatoriness of the Redeemer's merit, on the Supreme Being' or, that from God, as a just debt.[21]

Thus, the Edwardean reply to Universalism lay in the denial of the major proposition. They denied that Christ satisfied distributive justice.

The primary purpose of the Atonement was not to vindicate the law. Bellamy and Hopkins, as we have seen, make vindication of the law the central element in Atonement. Doctor Edwards, for example, objects strongly to the notion of vindication. He asserts in "The Necessity of the Atonement":

> If the obedience and death of Christ did prove that the law is just, still, by this circumstance, they would make no atonement for sin. If it were a truth that the obedience and death of Christ did prove the divine law to be just, and merely on that account made atonement, the ground of this truth would be, that whatever makes it manifest that the law is just, makes atonement. The essence of the atonement on this hypothesis, is placed in the manifestation of the justice of the divine law. Therefore this manifestation, however or by whomsoever it be made, is an atonement.[22]

In his "Essay on Atonement," Burge supports Doctor Edwards:

> For if the justice of a law be suspected, the justice of him who gave the law must be equally called in question; and, consequently, no conduct of his, founded on this suspicious law, can be considered as free from the same suspicion.[23]

Emmons speaks representatively when he declares in "The Purchase of Christ's Blood" that the Atonement was not effected on account of the sinners themselves. His development is illuminating.

> As sinners, they deserve to suffer the penalty of the law which they have broken; and God might have inflicted upon them eternal death which is the proper wages of sin. On the other hand, he might have saved them in a sovereign manner, without doing injustice to them, or to any other of his creatures. . . . If no atonement had been made, God might have treated them according to their deserts, or better than their deserts, without doing them, or any

> other creature, the least injury. . . . They see nothing, on their own account, why God may not exercise his justice or his grace towards them, without atonement. They know that he would not injure them, if he should exercise either justice or his grace towards them. Consequently, they see no need of an atonement on their own account. If no atonement had been made, God might have determined to destroy the human race, or to have saved all the human race, without doing injury to them, or any other created being. It hence appears that there was no necessity for the atonement of Christ, on account of sinners themselves.[24]

The Atonement was not necessary to demonstrate the reasonableness of the law and the capacity of man to obey it. Burge writes in his "Essay on the Atonement":

> Equally erroneous is the opinion that the atonement was necessary to show that the divine law may be obeyed by man. What Christ has done and suffered does not prove this. It is true, Christ obeyed the law; but how this can possibly afford any evidence that man is capable of obeying it, does not appear. For Christ was not a mere man.[25]

Obviously this statement by Burge is an attack upon Socinianism.

Attention should now be given to the positive declarations of the Edwardeans about the necessity of the Atonement. Extracts from several representatives will be given in order to demonstrate that there is common agreement among the Edwardeans on this point. Doctor Edwards inquires in "The Necessity of the Atonement":

> Why is an atonement necessary to the pardon of the

> sinner? I answer, it is necessary on the same ground, and for the same reason, as punishment would have been necessary, if there had been no atonement made. The ground of both is the same. The question then comes to this: Why should it have been necessary, if no statement had been made, that punishment should be inflicted on the transgressors of the divine law? This, I suppose, would have been necessary, to maintain the authority of the divine law. If that be not maintained, but the law fall into contempt, the contempt will fall equally on the legislator himself; his authority will be despised and his government weakened.[26]

In "A Discourse Designed to Explain the Doctrine of the Atonement," Maxcy declares:

> For if God should not execute the penalty endured by the transgressors, if he should not manifest in his moral government the same abhorrence of sin that he does in the declarations of the law, his word and his conduct would be repugnant to each other, and he would afford no convincing evidence, that his law was a transcript of his will; and that it ought to be considered as sacred, and respected as a universal, invariable standard of obedience for all rational creatures.[27]

Smalley asserts in "None but Believers Saved through the All-Sufficient Satisfaction of Christ":

> The thing was, sin could not be pardoned and sinners saved, consistently with just law and good government; and therefore not consistently with the glory of God or the good of the universe. The removal of this just obstacle to the reign of grace, not the laying God under obligation,

> for value received, was what rendered the redemption of Christ necessary; and the former of these, not the latter, is the end effected by his obedience and death.[28]

Weeks expresses the same idea of necessity in his "Dialogue":

> By his death the evil of sin has been made to appear in a light infinitely stronger than it ever could have appeared in the condemnation of the world. By so doing, he has magnified the law and made it honourable, although the execution of its threatening of death to the sinner is dispensed with. . . . The evils which would have followed from the pardon of the sinner without an atonement are effectually guarded against. And now, God can be just, just to himself, just to his own character as the righteous governor of the universe, and yet forgive sinners for Christ's sake.[29]

The Atonement was necessary, therefore, on God's account to display His aversion to sin. The true disposition of God toward evil would have been misunderstood if He had forgiven sin without this display. Misunderstanding would have resulted in chaos in His government. If the heinousness of sin be displayed or if God's regard for the law as a transcript of Himself be exhibited, forgiveness can thence be proffered with impunity. No one will think that God winks at sin or that infraction of the law will go unpunished. West, whose *Doctrine of the Atonement* we have examined, equally emphasizes the necessity of a display of God's determination to punish sin. This stress is distinguishable from Grotius' view by the very fact of this clear emphasis upon God's determination to punish sin.

There was no ontological necessity for Christ's satisfaction. A debt was not paid by Him. Distributive justice was not satisfied by Him. The ill desert of man remains and the law must still wound the offender unless the sovereign ruler by a special act of forgiveness lifts the penalty. The Atonement was necessary on God's account to display to the world by an unforgettable Gethsemane and a shameful cross that He abhors all evil and that no one can break the moral law without jeopardizing his own soul. The Atonement did not vindicate the law. Its righteousness or justness inheres in the character of the Lawgiver. The Atonement supports the law and the moral government by an unequivocal language of condemnation to offenders. Thus the Atonement is necessary on God's account for the good estate of His government. It is a functional but not an ontological necessity. This is an objective aspect of the Edwardean theory.

The Edwardeans stress also a subjective aspect. God's display of His aversion to sin is the most potent deterrent to sin. The cross is calculated to restrain sinful man and bring about obedience to the law. However, the Edwardeans fail to show that it has been a deterrent. In other words, they affirm that the cross has a deterring potency but they do not make explicit how, when, and where its potency has been manifested. Again one wonders why the subjective element is so strongly emphasized when it is solidly held that the elect are preserved by a sovereign grace.

IV. THE NATURE OF THE ATONEMENT

Before stating the Edwardean view on the nature of the Atonement it is necessary to give attention to the matters of justice and suffering.

The Edwardeans hold that sin and punishment have regard to distributive justice but the Atonement has regard to general justice. It is important to mark this. They recognize both distributive and general justice as operative principles. They reject commutative justice summarily.

Distributive justice is a moral principle. It has to do with reward and punishment. It is the language of deserts. From the standpoint of distributive justice humanity stands utterly condemned. The sanction of the law must be invoked. Condign and irremediable punishment must be meted out to man. It was pointed out in the preceding section of this chapter that man, alienated from God and condemned, is morally unable to repent and to obey. It was also pointed out that if man were morally able to repent, this act of repentance would be insufficient ground for God's forgiving him. The Atonement is necessary before God can forgive, for the Atonement opens the door to or removes the barrier from His mercy.

The Atonement, however, has nothing to do with the principle of distributive justice. The Edwardeans vehemently oppose the notion that the sins of man were imputed to Christ. The precise penalty threatened in the law was not invoked against Him. His suffering and death do not in and of themselves mitigate man's frightful status nor is man any less deserving of eternal death on account of Christ's passion. Forgiveness, if and when it is given, is purely a gracious act of God and it is in no *direct* way a consequence of Christ's satisfaction. Strictly speaking, the Atonement does not touch distributive justice at any point. It has absolutely nothing to do with God's gracious forgiveness of any soul. Forgiveness is a sovereign act which is neither motivated nor conditioned by the cross. But on the other hand, the cross has respect to the soul that is forgiven in several ways. It deepens the soul's humiliation and sorrow for sin and it heightens the soul's appreciation of God's holy aversion to sin and the soul's love of righteousness. This subjective value of the cross does not precede but follows regeneration, an act of God which is sovereignly applied to whomsoever He wills to elect. The cross has no objective value with respect to distributive justice. There is no ontological hindrance to God's forgiving a repentant soul. Atonement has respect to the general good of His moral government.

It is general justice which is satisfied by the Atonement. General justice has regard to the good estate of the moral government and to the highest good of man generally considered. God's broken law is honored and supported and His aversion to sin is displayed by means of Christ's passion.

These two facts should be underscored: (1) the penalty for sin according to distributive justice is condign punishment; and (2) Christ's passion is the means of satisfying general but not distributive justice. According to the threatening of the law man's demerits deserve punishment. By reason of the nature of sin and the declaration of God, the punishment for sin is eternal death. The Penal theory holds that Christ suffered the threatened penalty of the law. On the other hand, the Edwardeans say that Christ suffered but that He did not suffer the penalty under which man stood condemned. Christ's suffering of the penalty of sin, according to distributive justice, is related by the Edwardeans to general justice. The penalty in the first instance is eternal death but Christ did not suffer eternal death. How can suffering, which is the penalty for sin according to distributive justice, satisfy general justice? The answer to this question is the Edwardean conception of the nature of the Atonement.

Four important observations should be made about the suffering of Christ before the Edwardean view on the nature of the Atonement is stated. First, His suffering was unspeakably severe. It had to be. It was through Christ's suffering that God disclosed His real aversion to sin and his determination to support His broken law. Smalley asserts:

> Now by laying such amazing sufferings on his dearly beloved son—by its pleasing the Lord thus to bruise him, and put him to grief, the divine vindictive justice was more awfully, as well as more amiably manifested, than ever it could have been by the punishment of sinners themselves to all eternity. . . . Nothing could ever make the law appear so steadfast, or afford such full ground of faith that every transgression shall receive a just recompense of reward, as the bloody sweat, the deserted exclamation, the expiring agonies, of our Divine Saviour.[30]

Burge heartily agrees with Smalley's view. For example, Burge states:

> The sufferings of Christ constituted the most affecting scene which was ever exhibited on earth. His death was the most grand and awful event which the world ever witnessed. In view of it, the sun withheld his beams, and the heavens were clothed in mourning; the earth trembled, and the graves of the dead were opened. Nature sympathized with her suffering and dying Lord.[31]

Second, the Edwardeans maintain that it was necessary that Christ suffer publicly. Here we see the influence of Bellamy who in particular stressed the necessity of the public display of Christ's suffering. Griffin, among the Edwardeans, is especially emphatic on this point. He says that "nothing belongs to the Atonement but what is public."[32] The Atonement was not an *ab extra* transaction based upon a private covenant between the Father and the Son. It was of such nature that it had to be effected publicly. Obviously a display demands spectators. The Atonement was a display.

Third, Christ's suffering was not equivalent to that deserved by the elect. For example, Emmons maintains:

> Though he suffered in our stead, yet he did not suffer the punishment which we deserve, and which the law threatens to us. He never transgressed the law, and so the law could not threaten any punishment to him. His sufferings were by no means equal, in degree or duration, to the eternal sufferings that we deserve, and which God has threatened to inflict upon us. So that he did in no sense bear the penalty of the law, which we have broken and justly deserve.[33]

The Edwardeans do not attempt to establish a proportion between the quantity of Christ's suffering and that deserved by the elect. His suffering is not commensurate to theirs with respect either to quantity or quality. It is important to bear this in mind. The Edwardeans are careful to say that His suffering was unfeigned and severe. That declaration is basic to their theory but any semblance of a *quid pro quo* proportion is disavowed.

Fourth, it should be observed that the purpose of all suffering is to display God's attitude toward the holy law. Since the law is a transcript of Himself, His attitude toward those who break it is a disclosure of His nature. Vindictive justice is a glorious attribute. The pains of Christ were pleasing to the Father. Doctor Edwards asserts:

> It has been said, that it is incredible that mere pain should be agreeable to a God of infinite goodness; that therefore the sufferings of Christ were agreeable to God only as a proof of the strength of the virtue of Christ, or of his disposition to obey the divine law. If by mere pain be meant pain abstracted from the obedience of Christ, I cannot see why it may not be agreeable to God. It certainly is in the damned; and for the same reason might have been, and doubtless was, in the case of our Lord. The

Father was pleased with the pains of his Son, as they were necessary to support the authority of his law and government, in the salvation of sinners.[34]

We are now prepared to state the nature of the Atonement as it is conceived by the Edwardeans. Christ's suffering was substituted for the penalty of the law because it was equivalent in meaning to that which had been threatened. This is not Scotus' theory of acceptilation. Nothing was offered to God, not even a token, in the suffering of Christ. The Edwardeans reject everything that hints of imputation. Equivalence, which connotes some quantity or quality of suffering in lieu of the elects' deserved punishment, is likewise rejected. Equivalence has regard to the meaning of Christ's suffering and only to that. Suffering displays divine abhorrence to sin. Suffering honors God's broken law.

The Edwardeans insist that "free" grace is inconsistent with the view that Christ satisfied commutative or distributive justice. Thus the Edwardeans did not support the view previously held by President Edwards and the New England Calvinists. President Edwards had said that salvation is an absolute debt to the believer inasmuch as forgiveness and reward have been purchased by Christ's satisfaction and merit. This was also the view of the New England Calvinists. The Edwardeans rejected that notion. Since Christ has not satisfied commutative or distributive justice, forgiveness is an act of grace.

It is true that President Edwards looked upon the Atonement as a work of pure grace. God initiated and conducted it. However, after God's justice had been satisfied, He was obliged to bestow the benefits of Christ's passion and merit upon the elect. But this obligation rested in turn upon a gratuitous promise. The grace of God thus was prior to and also in the act of Atonement. After the Atonement was finished, He was bound by His promise to bestow its benefits upon the elect. On the other hand, the Edwardeans hold that grace is a free act which is subsequent to but not consequent upon the suffering of Christ. This calls for elucidation. They did not deny that grace is prior to the Atonement, for it was a voluntary decision of God to remove the barrier to His mercy. But the gift of grace is subsequent to the suffering of Christ. Before God could safely offer grace it was necessary for Him to exhibit His aversion to sin and His regard for the broken law. This was necessary for Himself as the moral governor and for the highest good of His subjects. Since Atonement has been accomplished, He can bestow grace with impunity upon whomsoever He elects. The essential difference, however, between President Edwards and his successors on this point is not a matter of the time element—whether prior to or subsequent to Christ's suffering. The essential difference lies in the nature of the Atonement. The Edwardeans hold that grace is not consequent upon the Atonement. Christ's suffering did not satisfy distributive justice. The ill desert of the elect was not removed by His passion. They will remain ill-deserving forever, despite the fact that they have repented. The Atonement merely precludes a false impression of God's real attitude toward Himself as holy and toward His law as a transcript of Himself. The locus of the barrier to grace is in the subjects but not in the governor. Edwards put the barrier in the justice of God, in His nature. The promised grace was therefore contingent upon the eternal determination that Christ suffer and die for the sins of the elect.

From the practical point of view, it is immaterial when and how grace becomes operative so long as God's absolute sovereignty is the only efficient factor in conducting and applying the Atonement.

The Edwardeans appear to make Christ's suffering a mere

display, a ghastly exhibition. He suffered as an innocent person. In no sense was it deserved. He was not actually bearing the sins of the elect for no sin was imputed to Him. However, the efficacy of the suffering of Christ does not depend upon the impression that it makes upon man in general, even though the Edwardeans affirm the deterring potency in His suffering.

Assuming that suffering displays divine aversion to sin, is this the only means by which it can be displayed? Does not obedience to the law as well as suffering display God's true disposition? The Edwardeans do not look upon Christ's obedience as constituting a part of the Atonement. Obedience was necessary as a precondition to the efficacy of His suffering. It procures a reward for those who are united with Christ as clients with their patron.

It is a moot question whether the sanctity of the law is disclosed more clearly by the suffering of a criminal than by the obedience of a good subject. It is also a moot question whether the generality of subjects is greater influenced for good by the punishment of lawbreakers or by the obedience of well-disciplined subjects. It seems to the present writer that the Edwardeans are guilty of an important omission in failing to make Christ's obedience as prominent a factor as suffering in the Atonement. There is no reason for not combining the two, for both would tend to support the law which, according to the Edwardeans, is a transcript of God's nature.

V. THE EXTENT OF THE ATONEMENT

In advocating the doctrine of General Atonement the exponents of the Edwardean theory were acting consistently with their position as to the necessity and nature of the

Atonement. However, when it is said that these Edwardeans with one accord taught the doctrine of General Atonement, it is incumbent that we understand the import of "general." The term has three connotations to which attention should be given.

First, it may signify that Christ's satisfaction in its nature and its efficacy effects the complete and ultimate restoration of all mankind. Clearly this is not meant by the Edwardeans. They strenously object to Universalism and hold that it is for the glory of God and the highest good of the universe that some souls be damned.

Second, General Atonement may signify that forgiveness of sins can be universally proclaimed on the condition of faith. This implies that whatever means of grace God may use with one He will use with all who hear the gospel. There is clear evidence that the Edwardeans hold that a general proclamation of the gospel should be made and that whoever hears is urged to believe God's offer and comply with the gospel terms. Smalley says: "A door of salvation is set open to all men. Whosoever will is heartily bid welcome to take of the water of life freely."[35]

Emmons declares:

> The atonement of Christ has the same favorable aspect upon the non-elect as upon the elect. It opens as wide a door of mercy to the one as to the other. It removes all natural obstacles out of the way of the salvation of either, because it renders it consistent with the justice of God to pardon and save a part, or the whole of mankind, according to His sovereign pleasure and eternal purpose.[36]

Despite these unequivocal declarations about "general", it must be said that this is not what the doctrine of General Atonement amounts to in its final analysis.

Third, atonement is general in the sense that God is now free to act sovereignly in electing souls for salvation. That is, the broken law has been so honored and God's aversion to sin has been so displayed through Christ's suffering that whatever God may do by way of forgiving sinful man cannot henceforth bring disrepute to Him as the moral Governor or bring moral chaos to His dominion. Burge speaks representatively in declaring:

> But though the atonement is, strictly speaking for all mankind, one as much as another, this does not imply any obligation on the part of God, either to Christ or to sinners, to save any of them. Notwithstanding the atonement, God is at full liberty to save, or not to save, just as the general good may require, and his unerring wisdom dictate. If the general good require that any of these for whom Christ died should be left to continue in impenitency, and to perish in their sins, God may thus leave them, in perfect consistency with the nature and design of the atonement.[37]

This is quite a different matter from that of universal proclamation and authentic invitation. The doctrine of election as it is held by the Edwardeans involves a special and more potent grace upon the elect than upon the nonelect. All who receive this special grace are saved and all who do not receive it are damned. God Himself solely determines who shall and who shall not receive this grace. There is nothing inherently good in those chosen to commend them to the favor of God, and there is nothing more inherently evil in the condemned to merit His disfavor of them. All stand on the same moral place. All are sinful, alienated, and under condemnation. Election is purely a matter of inscrutable choice.

The doctrine of General Atonement means simply that a general or universal bar to God's mercy has been removed by Christ's satisfaction of general justice. Since God's broken law has been honored and the integrity of His moral government has been protected, He can act sovereignly and rescue whomsoever He wills to save from the threatened perils of eternal death. When God acts sovereignly in electing souls, is He really acting as the moral governor or as the Sovereign God? When He sovereignly acts in forgiving the elect He is not relaxing the penalty on account of Christ's suffering. Forgiveness is a sovereign act of mercy in spite of the law and its threatenings. The Edwardeans clearly affirm that the suffering of Christ was substituted for the penalty of the law. However, no *individual soul* is elected because Christ's suffering is substituted for the punishment *that soul* deserves. Election is the act of the Sovereign dealing with specific souls. In a general way the suffering of Christ is substituted for the penalty of the law. The penalty of the law is to display God's abhorrence of sin. Christ's suffering displays this abhorrence. There is the substitution of a display for a display. However, a substitution of a display for a display is neither the ground of God's mercy nor the controlling factor in His disposing of individual souls. According to the Edwardean scheme, the moral Governor who metes out justice according to strict moral deserts finally abdicates and the sovereign God mounts the throne.

Chapter 6

A CRITICAL RETROSPECT

Our analysis of the doctrine of the Atonement in Jonathan Edwards and his successors has disclosed five distinct theories. A brief recapitulation of these, with critical comments, should precede a comparative study of them.

I. RECAPITULATION OF PRESIDENT EDWARDS' THEORY

The scheme of President Edwards presupposes the necessity of a reconciliation of God's justice with His mercy as the precondition of forgiveness. This was not novel with him. Expressions of that necessity are found as early as the Patristic period. Protestant Scholasticism developed the idea to its most extreme limit in the Penal theory.

The Penal theory was a sacred element in President Edwards' theological heritage. More than a hundred years of faithful adherence had made it an indigenous factor in New England culture, the taproot of which was a definite religious ideology. There is no reason to doubt President

Edwards' reverence for a doctrine which was redolent of the piety of his forefathers. His modifications of it derive from his religious experience and exegesis of the Bible rather than from an iconoclastic bent.

President Edwards modified the Penal theory at two basic points. First, he abandoned the view of a rigid *quid pro quo* between Christ's passion and the suffering man deserved. This modification does not derive from a conviction that moral and spiritual matters do not yield to computation or from a conviction that suffering is highly personal and private. These are more recently developed views. President Edwards' modification of equivalence is a correlate of his appraisal of the dignity of Christ. The emphasis thus is shifted by him from the quantum of suffering Christ bore to the nature of Him who bore it and to the relation of the bearer to God. Because of His divine nature Christ was capable of experiencing a quality of suffering which is precluded to finite man. It was His Father's love for the Son which put the final appraisal upon His suffering. Thus, distributive justice was not satisfied by a precise endurance of the literal penalty of the law.

President Edwards introduced the idea that God is sovereign in applying as well as in originating and conducting the Atonement. Consequently, the Atonement is efficacious for him for whom alone it was arbitrarily intended. This does not mean that the extent of its impact is circumscribed by sovereign election. It means that the Atonement does not make an impact at all. God elects specific souls. These are illumined by an irresistible and irrevocable grace. Their faith is not a response to the Atonement *per se,* although it is the necessary complement to the Atonement. It completes the Atonement as remanation completes emanation.

According to President Edwards, Christ's work *per se* does not affect man. In the final analysis, it does not deal with man's predicament. President Edwards' doctrine of the Atonement is a contrivance to mesh God's attributes with the doctrine of sovereign election. President Edwards held that all God's attributes are functional. None can fail of expression. Vindictive justice is an indispensable attribute. It cannot be manifested if there are no sinners. Therefore, God decrees sin. He demands that all sinners must die. This is an inviolable decree. Some sinners do suffer eternal death. Their punishment is a glorious fact for it affords God the occasion to manifest an indispensable facet of His nature. But God is merciful, too. His mercy cannot contravene His justice. To exercise mercy which must be exercised He elects some souls upon whom He will show it. However, His irrevocable word is that the sinner must die. Christ comes under the elects' sin and suffers and dies for them. No, not for them! He suffers the penalty in order that all God's attributes may be effectually functional and compatible.

There are two emphases in President Edwards' thought to which special attention should be paid. First, he grounds the moral law in the character of God. Since it is thus grounded, it is just as immutable as His character. President Edwards does not make a distinction between the immutability of the law and the immutability of its sanction. Both inhere in the very nature of God. Second, President Edwards makes love the all-controlling attribute of God. Justice, mercy, truth, faithfulness—in short, all His attributes—are delineations of love. The end of love is God Himself. Every propensity to emanate Himself is also a propensity to Himself as the end. The very nature of love demands expression or, to state it differently, it is essential to His nature that He diffuse Himself. Therefore, whatever occurs is both an expression of His love and a glorification of it. The empirical fact of an event is sure evidence both that He willed it and that it is good. Election and damnation are indispensable and glorious expressions of His nature, of His love, on this ground.

It is quite likely that President Edwards' idea of love as the all-controlling attribute of God suggested to his successors that the moral governor rules with the highest good of His government in view. If it did not suggest the idea, it undoubtedly supported it.

II. RECAPITULATION OF BELLAMY'S THEORY

THE THEORY OF Bellamy turns on the pivot of vindication. He abandons the notion of equivalence for the most part, although he does not extricate himself entirely from it. There are passages in his *Works* which unmistakably teach Christ's satisfaction of distributive justice. Therein lies an obvious inconsistency, for he clearly affirms that the mission of Christ did not have this end in view. It was for the specific purpose of vindicating the just and holy law. Vindication was effected by means of Christ's obedience unto death. His obedience is a testimony to the justness of the law itself and of the condemnation threatened therein. The suffering of Christ is not magnified. It was attendant to His obedience unto death. It was merely the sign of the unswerving intention of God to punish sin. Christ's suffering does not expiate sin. Suffering *per se* is not an Atonement. Thus, the old notion of equivalence is rejected. Atonement is effected when the law is adequately vindicated.

Bellamy introduces the idea of General Atonement into New England thought. It is imperative that we do not mistake his meaning here. He does affirm that Christ died for all mankind. He urges the universal proclamation of the gospel on this ground. However, it might be maintained that he nullifies the general efficacy of the gospel by his declaration of sovereign election. He goes so far as to say that the Atonement was not designed for the nonelect. He holds with President Edwards that the vindictive justice of God is a glorious attribute which must be manifested. The condemnation of the nonelect is a necessary expression of the divine character. Unrepented sin becomes an indispensable element in the universal scheme, for without it the nature of God would fail of expression. Therefore, it would seem that the universal proclamation of the gospel would be contrary to the sovereign intention of God.

The framework of Bellamy's theory is rectoral. This is a likely influence of Grotius. Bellamy urges that God rules by law. His is a moral government. The glory of God and the highest good of the universe are denominated the ends of His government. This twofold expression of ends actually connotes one end. That end is God Himself, for the highest good of the universe is tantamount to the highest glory of God. Although Bellamy's phraseology here differs from that of President Edwards', the former does not deviate from the latter's idea about God's last end in creation. Parenthetically, a question should be interjected at this point. Does Bellamy's view of the highest good of the universe, generally considered, preserve the values of each soul? Our attention will be directed to this question later.

The governmental framework soon dominated thought on the Atonement in New England. The attractiveness of the view may reflect the late eighteenth-century social and political milieu. That was the period in which nascent strivings for democracy, justice, and legal rights were being felt throughout New England. Given their stress upon God as the moral governor who rules by law, the governmental framework appears somewhat awkward because Bellamy and the other advocates of it were too steeped in their theological heritage, a heritage which was completely subservient to the idea of absolute sovereignty. However careful they were to develop the governmental scheme, they did not emancipate themselves from the idea that God rules according to His sovereign, inscrutable, and arbitrary will.

III. RECAPITULATION OF HOPKINS' THEORY

Hopkins' scheme follows Bellamy's in many particulars. He grounds law in the character of God. God rules by a just and holy law. He is the moral governor. General Atonement is affirmed. Hopkins, like Bellamy, seems to vitiate both the idea that God is the moral governor and that the Atonement is general. It is his view on sovereignty that does this. Here he duplicates the view of President Edwards and Bellamy.

The pivot of the Atonement is the vindication of the law. Although Bellamy, too, made this the matter of the Atonement, Hopkins' idea of vindication stands in opposition to the former's. Vindication for Hopkins is effected by Christ's suffering. It cannot be effected in any other way for suffering is in every instance the evidence of God's regard for His immutable law. The suffering of Christ is a manifestation which allows no misconstruction. It expresses one clear message to the world: God's law is just and its infraction brings swift, sure, and just punishment.

The ultimate end in Christ's vindication is the protection of the moral government of God. Christ's suffering does not pay a debt or satisfy distributive justice. The status of man is not altered thereby, nor is his ill desert removed on its account. His suffering removes the possibility of misinterpretation of God's regard for His law and of His intention to punish the disobedient. When the law is thus vindicated God's mercy toward the elect can be shown with impunity.

Atonement is consummated by a sufficient vindication. Christ's suffering is sufficient for that.

Hopkins' emphasis upon suffering is a clear influence of President Edwards. His ideas of moral government, vindication, and General Atonement mark his affinity with Bellamy. An instability in Hopkins' thought derives from the combination of mutually incompatible ideas in his scheme. It is clear that his depiction of Christ's suffering can infer only one thing, an equivalence. An equivalence can be properly correlated only with commutative or distributive justice. Hopkins correlates it with general justice. He insists that Christ's suffering was primarily spiritual. He fails to stress that it was publicly displayed. The essence of vindication lies in public manifestation. Bellamy is correct in his emphasis upon this factor; that is, if vindication is the matter of the Atonement.

IV. RECAPITULATION OF WEST'S THEORY

West strengthens the line of development from President Edwards to the Edwardeans. His view on law and its sanctions stems definitely from President Edwards. He supports Bellamy and Hopkins in advocating the governmental view and General Atonement. However, he tends to undermine his structure by affirming the absolute sovereignty of God in applying the Atonement.

On the other hand, West breaks the line of development from President Edwards to his successors. The irregular element in his view lies in his return to the doctrine of imputation. In this respect he is not a successor of President Edwards. If he had not advocated imputation, it would be correct to say that his is the full-fledged Edwardean theory of the Atonement, for it is only in this matter that a vital difference appears between his view and that of the Edwardeans. It is correct to assert that West's view is a combination of the Penal theory and the governmental concept. In that lies its anomalous nature.

West holds that the Atonement is an exhibition. God's abhorrence of evil is displayed in the passion of Christ. The significance of the display derives from the reality of Christ's expiation of sin. The Edwardeans also make display the central element in the Atonement. However, according to their view Christ's suffering does not signify expiation. West conceived of Christ's suffering as the result of His actual bearing of imputed sin. His suffering was a genuine equivalence of the deserved punishment of the elect. It was a real, punitive satisfaction. As sunrays display the reality of the sun, Christ's suffering exhibited the reality of His interchange with the sinful elect. Nevertheless, West fails to apply this point of view. He rejects the notion that Christ satisfied distributive justice and relates suffering to general justice. He holds that Atonement is effected when God manifests His aversion to sin, and that nothing short of an infinite suffering is an adequate manifestation. An expiation does manifest an aversion. This accords with the Penal theory. But West's logic fails here. Although manifestation is the counterpart of expiation, nevertheless Christ did not expiate sin. He exhibited divine abhorrence to sin and thus opened the way for God to forgive whomsoever He elects without jeopardizing His good name and His moral government.

V. RECAPITULATION OF THE EDWARDEAN THEORY

THE EDWARDEAN THEORY is a composite of elements drawn from the theories of President Edwards, Bellamy,

Hopkins, and West. The most obvious distinction of the Edwardean theory lies in its novel interpretation of the suffering of Christ. Special attention will be given shortly to this interpretation.

The Edwardeans follow their predecessors in grounding law in the character of God. They concur in the opinion that sanctions are indispensable to law. However, they insist that the penalty threatened in the law is relaxable. President Edwards himself had held that the penalty must be enforced. It was on this ground that he maintained the necessity of an equivalence between the suffering of Christ and that deserved by the elect. Although Bellamy and Hopkins are not explicit on this point, their theories presuppose that the penalty may be relaxed by means of an adequate satisfaction. Satisfaction for them meant vindication. The Edwardeans, on the other hand, make display the matter of satisfaction.

The nature of display as conceived by the Edwardeans calls for careful statement. West, too, made this the central idea in his scheme. However, the term does not connote the same thing for West as for the Edwardeans. West taught the sins of the elect were imputed to Christ. Consequently, display for him connoted the external complement of an internal expiation. The Edwardeans, on the other hand, reject outright the notion of imputation. The suffering of Christ did not come upon Him through the expiation of sin. Therefore, the suffering He bore was merely a display—a display without a material counterpart. Christ, the innocent Son of God, was a penal example of what God will certainly do to all who do not repent. His suffering does not vindicate the law. It honors and supports the broken law. It is calculated to restrain man from sinning. Atonement is consummated when God's true disposition toward sin is adequately displayed, for thenceforth God can exercise mercy toward the elect without endangering His honor as the moral governor.

The distinguishing mark in the Edwardean theory lies in the stress upon Christ's suffering without its being an expiation. The stress President Edwards, Hopkins, and West put upon suffering is repeated by the Edwardeans. It is scarcely possible to depict suffering in more gruesome terms than they have done. In fact, the more gruesome their description of suffering, the more precise they are in presenting their view. If one admits the ontological necessity for the satisfaction of distributive justice as the prerequisite of God's offer of mercy, he will see a justification for the attempt to depict Christ's suffering as unspeakably horrible. But this necessity is summarily rejected by the Edwardeans. The sinless Christ is subjected to shame and pain by the Father! The Father makes an example of His only-begotten Son who knew no sin and who did not actually bear the sins of others! Such a view, it might be urged, would not restrain sin but provoke hearty disgust for the moral governor.

The Edwardeans reflect the influence of Bellamy by their espousal of the governmental concept and General Atonement. They are true to President Edwards, Bellamy, Hopkins, and West with respect to the sovereignty of God in applying the Atonement.

VI. VARYING VIEWS ON NECESSITY FOR ATONEMENT

With respect to the necessity of the Atonement, three views have appeared in the doctrines we have examined. First, President Edwards maintained that it was necessary for the penalty for sin to be borne by Christ before God could consistently forgive man. Thus, he affirmed the necessity of the satisfaction of distributive justice. Second, Bellamy and Hopkins rejected President Edwards' view of expiation.

They held that the law must be vindicated as the precondition to forgiveness. They reasoned in this manner: it would endanger God's moral government if He forgave sin without first giving to man an unforgettable proof of His regard for the just and holy law and of His determination to visit the disobedient with condign punishment. Having vindicated the law, no one could ever believe He winks at sin or that vindictiveness is not an attribute of His nature. Consequently, vindication opens the door to, or removes the bar from, His mercy. Third, West and the Edwardeans made exhibition or display the key word. The purpose of the Atonement according to them is quite like that expressed by Bellamy and Hopkins. However, there is a clear distinction between vindication and exhibition. Vindication is a testimony in support of the justness and rightness of the law. Exhibition presumes that the law needs no vindication. If it is not adjudged to be just and right, neither Christ's obedience nor His suffering can alter man's appraisal of it. Exhibition has regard to the support and honoring of the law. It is a revelation of divine abhorrence against those who insolently disobey. The adequate display of divine aversion to evil, so the Edwardeans maintain, opens the door to, or removes the bar from, God's mercy.

VII. VARYING VIEWS ON NATURE OF ATONEMENT

THERE ARE FIVE distinct views on the nature of the Atonement in the theories we have examined. First, President Edwards held that the Atonement consists in the expiation of sin by means of Christ's suffering. He deviates from the Penal view only with respect to the connotation of equivalence. He maintained that Christ did not suffer the literal penalty of the law, but suffered "as He was capable of." The dignity of the bearer is the ultimate index to God's appraisal of the quantity and quality of vicarious suffering. Second, Bellamy affirmed that the Atonement consists of the vindication of the law by means of Christ's obedience unto death. Third, although Hopkins concurs in Bellamy's view of the necessity of vindication, the former's view of the nature of the Atonement differs from that of the latter. Hopkins magnifies the suffering of Christ and maintains that vindication was consummated by means of it. Fourth, West held that the Atonement was an exhibition of divine abhorrence against sin. It is important to recall that for him exhibition was the counterpart of expiation. Here the affinity of West's view with the Penal theory is apparent. Fifth, the view of the Edwardeans is like West's, with one salient exception: they made exhibition central, but divested it of expiation. That is, Christ's suffering was a mere display, a penal example. It was not the effect of His actually bearing imputed sin.

VIII. COMMON AND DIVERGENT ELEMENTS IN THE VARIOUS THEORIES

THE ADVOCATES OF the five theories we have studied hold four salient elements in common. First, each grounded his theory in the concept of the law as an expression of God's nature. The law as such is neither arbitrary nor alterable. Its character inheres in the character of the just and holy Lawgiver. Bellamy originated the expression "a transcript of God" in speaking of the law. His phrase was literally adopted by West and the Edwardeans. Second, all conceive of love as the all-controlling attribute of God. This will be commented upon in another context. Third, there is unanimity in making Christ's passion the whole matter of the Atonement. His obedience was not adjudged to be a part of the Atonement itself. It was merely a qualification of the Redeemer. Fourth, there is perfect agreement as to the sovereignty of God in applying the Atonement.

It is obvious that the *terminus a quo* and the *terminus ad quem* are identical in all these theories. Each is grounded in law as a transcript of God and each comes finally to the espousal of sovereignty in applying the Atonement. Their thought-routes differ. Some take a direct route, others follow a labyrinthine trail, but all come to the same destination. All re-establish the Calvinistic sovereign God upon the throne and coronate Him anew.

It is evident that there are direct lines from the theory of President Edwards to the Edwardean view. Are these lines of such major importance as to warrant the assertion that President Edwards' teachings supported the theory of his successors? In answering this question, it is important to evaluate these connecting lines. A distinction must be made between the elements which determine the framework and those which form the vital substance of a theory. The nature of law, love as the all-controlling attribute of God, Christ's passion as the whole substance of the Atonement, and sovereignty in applying the Atonement are matters which determine the framework of a theory of the Atonement. These are not the vital factors in the theory itself. But these are the elements which mark the affinity of President Edwards' theory with that of the Edwardeans.

The vital elements in a theory are the necessity, nature, and extent of the Atonement. On these three points there is a wide difference between President Edwards and his successors. President Edwards developed his theory from the perspective of an ontological necessity for the satisfaction of distributive justice. Although he modified the old notion of *quid pro quo,* he did not disavow the necessity of an equivalence between the elects' deserved suffering and that which Christ endured. He explicitly taught expiation of sin by means of Christ's suffering of condign punishment at the hand of God. The Edwardeans stressed suffering, but they strongly objected to the idea of Christ's satisfaction of distributive justice. On the matter of the necessity of the Atonement, they stood in opposition to President Edwards. Moreover, our analysis of President Edwards' theory has not disclosed any evidence which would warrant the opinion that the Edwardeans found support from his view on necessity.

President Edwards held that the Atonement consists in Christ's bearing the sins of the elect. This is a corollary of his view about the necessity of the Atonement. The Edwardeans insisted that the nature of the Atonement consists in a display of divine abhorrence of sin. Undoubtedly, President Edwards would have concurred in the opinion that Christ's suffering displayed divine abhorrence, but his demur would have been forthcoming to the notion that the Atonement was a mere display without the counterpart of satisfaction of distributive justice. Thus, on this essential matter there is a wide difference in point of view. It can safely be asserted that there is nothing in President Edwards' writings to support the Edwardeans with respect to the nature of the Atonement.

It has been shown that President Edwards taught Limited Atonement. Park, as has been pointed out, said that President Edwards seemed to favor General Atonement in passages here and there. However, Park failed to cite any of these passages in support of his contention. The present writer said, in commenting on Park's assertion, that the evidence for that declaration is more inferential than explicit. President Edwards did write an approving preface to Bellamy's *True Religion Delineated,* in which General

Atonement is espoused. It was shown how President Edwards might well have done so without surrendering his own view. It was also pointed out that Bellamy's explicit avowal of General Atonement finally yielded to his view on sovereignty. He at last declared that the Atonement was not designed for the nonelect.

The Edwardeans are clear in their espousal of General Atonement. They are not guilty, as was Bellamy, of saying that the Atonement was not designed for the nonelect. Nevertheless, by definitely committing themselves regarding God's sovereignty in applying the Atonement, they seem to vitiate the practical importance of their espousal of General Atonement. Thus, by their insistence upon the doctrine of General Atonement, the Edwardeans stood in opposition to President Edwards.

The conclusion is warranted that the Edwardeans find support in President Edwards for those elements which constitute the framework of the theory. With respect to those elements which form the vital substance of an Atonement theory, the evidence is such as to warrant the conclusion that the Edwardean theory does not lie either in the affirmations or in the nuances of President Edwards.

Stress upon vindication and exhibition implies stress upon the subjective efficacy of Christ's work. It is exceedingly irregular that the Edwardeans give so little attention to the application of this aspect. That the passion of Christ is calculated to deter from sinning is clearly and repeatedly affirmed. But the sheer assertion stands unsupported. It is not maintained by the present writer that empirical evidence for the subjective worth of Christ's work is wanting. The point is that our advocates of vindication and exhibition fail to adduce evidence to substantiate their declarations. On the other hand, it would seem to be unnecessary to insist upon the subjective value of vindication and exhibition while holding a rigid view of sovereign election and of its implications: special, irresistible, and irrevocable grace.

It is the opinion of the present writer that the theories we have reviewed are faulty in that they do not recognize Christ's obedience as a material element in the Atonement. For example, assuming that vindication or exhibition is the essence of the Atonement, it may be urged that obedience to the law is as necessary as suffering for vindication or exhibition.

President Edwards and his successors make love the all-controlling attribute of God. Since this is the case, all His actions emanate from love. It is not in the principle but in its application that fault is to be found. Beginning with Bellamy, the governmental scheme was advocated, according to which the governor always rules with the highest good of his government in view. Undoubtedly it is praiseworthy of a ruler to make this an objective. However, it must be said that our advocates of the governmental view fail to do justice to persons and personal values. There are several bases for this charge.

The necessity of sin is affirmed so that God may express all His attributes. Vindictive justice is an attribute. Therefore, there must be sinners, unforgiven sinners and eternally condemned sinners. Without them, God's nature could not be fully manifested. This idea is nothing short of disturbing, especially in the face of the affirmation of love. If God creates souls, decrees sin, arbitrarily refuses to elect some souls and sentences the nonelect to an eternal hell *for the sake of giving expression to an attribute of His nature which is love,* could He be respected as the moral governor? Moreover, it is affirmed that the rapture of the elect will be enhanced by their knowledge of the frightful judgment of God upon the nonelect. It is unnecessary to comment on this sadistic view. Suffice it to say that a moral governor and the elect members of his domain must at least be moral. It is one thing to hold that God's glory should be the supreme end. It is quite another thing to hold that He is glorified by wreaking vindictive justice upon souls created for condemnation.

There are two especially important lessons to be learned from the attempts of President Edwards and his successors to form a theory of the Atonement. First, a warning is contained in them for anyone who tries to develop a theory which is compatible with a rigid view of sovereignty in applying the Atonement. We have observed that every one of these New England theologians comes to the same conclusion, the same *cul-de-sac*. It matters not what one may urge regarding the nature, necessity, and extent of the Atonement, if the scheme finally yields to the doctrine of absolute sovereignty in its application. The practicality of a theory is thereby nullified. Within a framework of absolute sovereignty, any theory will deserve the ultimate judgment that it is neither *Christus pro nobis* nor *Christus in nobis* but *Christus pro deo*. Where this is the case its vitality as a moral and spiritual force is lost. Second, it is imperative that the doctrine of the Atonement be stated so as not to undermine other doctrines. With the possible exception of Bellamy, all our theologians cast suspicions upon their conception of the Trinity. It is especially encumbent upon one who holds the doctrine of the Trinity to beware of setting the attributes of the Father in opposition to those of the Son. It has been pointed out that this doctrine must be both coherent and moral. A contrariety between the Father's attributes and those of the Son undermines both essential tests of that doctrine.

Although it is beyond the scope of this book to trace the influence of President Edwards and his successors upon later developments of thought on the Atonement, it may be well to state two facts of historic interest and importance. First, President Edwards definitely suggested to McLeod Campbell his basic point of view: Christ's sympathetic union with man. Campbell's theory had a considerable vogue, especially in England. Second, the doctrine of the Atonement in Jonathan Edwards and his successors marks a transition from the Old New England view to Horace Bushnell and American advocates of the Subjective theory. All aspects of theology were in ferment in New England during three-quarters of the eighteenth century. The nascent strivings of liberalism are seen in the debate on anthropology, virtue, and moral agency which President Edwards provoked between 1730 and 1758. Although he did not foresee the results of his innovations with respect to the Atonement, they were portentous of a rejection of the Old New England view. That rejection came swiftly. Once a fissure is made in a dam the pressure of the harnessed water will relentlessly demand its enlargement. Soon the rushing current will become uncontrollable. The theological current, empounded by Old Calvinism and unleashed by President Edwards and his successors, proved to be a nemesis. The structure President Edwards built, in which his successors lived in separate but adjacent rooms, was finally carried away by the deluge.

FOOTNOTES

CHAPTER 1

1. Jonathan Edwards, *Works,* in eight volumes (London: James Black and Son, 1817). Jonathan Edwards, *Works,* in four volumes (New York: Robert Carter and Brothers, 1881). (Unless otherwise specified, all citations from Edwards' Works will be taken from latter edition, and will be given as follows: subject of sermon or treatise, volume, and page.)

2. See also Edwards A. Park, "Remarks of Jonathan Edwards on the Trinity," *Bibliotheca Sacra,* edited by Edwards A. Park (Andover: Warren F. Draper, 1881). XXXVIII, 147-187.

3. *Freedom of the Will,* II, 27.

4. *End in Creation,* II, 255.

5. *God's Sovereignty,* IV, 549.

6. Edited as *God Glorified in Man's Dependence,* IV, 169-178.

7. *Decrees and Election,* II, 522, 528.

8. *Decrees and Election,* II, 542.

9. *Decrees and Election,* II, 529.

10. *Freedom of the Will,* II, 179.

11. *Efficacious Grace,* II, 566.

12. *The Excellency of Christ,* IV, 179-201; see also *Pressing into the Kingdom of God,* IV, 381-402; *Ruth's Resolution,* IV, 412-421; *God the Best Portion of the Christian,* IV, 540-547.

13. *Religious Affections,* III, 5.

14. *Miscellaneous Observations,* I, 584.

15. *Decrees and Election,* II, 519.

16. *The Nature of True Virtue,* II, 261-304.

17. *End in Creation,* II, 222, 224, and 225.

18. *Decrees and Election,* II, 516, 517.

19. *Decrees and Election,* II, 516.

20. *Decrees and Election,* II, 516.

21. *Miscellaneous Observations,* I, 587f.

22. *Miscellaneous Observations,* I, 607.

23. *Decrees and Election,* II, 516.

24. *Pardon for the Greatest Sinners,* IV, 424; *Mysteries of Scripture,* III, 542.

25. *Miscellaneous Observations,* I, 584.

26. See also *Memoirs of President Edwards, Works,* I, 45.

27. The following are his most noteworthy polemic treatises:

Justification by Faith Alone (1734), a sermon which was expanded into a treatise for publication: against practical tendencies in Arminianism, IV, 64-132.

A Treatise Concerning Religious Affections (published 1746), a reply to Charles Chauncy's *Some Seasonable Thoughts on the State of Religion in New England* (1743): a defense of revivalism, III, 1-228.

Qualifications for Full Communion (1750), a defense of his stand against Stoddardeanism, I, 83-192.

Freedom of the Will (1754), a philosophical treatise against Arminianism, II, 1-182.

Original Sin Defended (1758), in particular a reply to Dr. John Taylor's *The Scriptural Doctrine of Original Sin Proposed to Free and Candid Examination* (1740), II, 305-510.

For an illuminating discussion of Edwards' polemical career, see Hugh Foster, *A Genetic History of the New England Theology,* pp. 51, 103.

28. *Religious Affections,* III, 102.

29. Since Edwards' theory of original sin excludes the loss of free-will, I have designated Adam's state as "not prejudiced." Relating will to choice and maintaining against Arminianism that one never chooses from indifference, Edwards held that free-will was not lost in the fall. Improper motivation and sinful desires—stuff out of which choices are made—misdirect the free-will. Obviously, while the term "free-will" is rescued, an ineluctable determinism is maintained.

30. *Justification by Faith Alone,* IV, 93.

31. *Justification by Faith Alone,* IV, 66.

32. *Justification by Faith Alone,* IV, 74.

33. *Original Sin,* II, 341, 348, 372, and 478.

34. *Efficacious Grace,* II, 569.

35. A term frequently used. See also *Wisdom Displayed in Salvation,* IV, 133-138.

36. *Work of Redemption,* I, 298.

37. *Work of Redemption,* I, 306-396.

38. *Wisdom Displayed in Salvation,* IV, 135-139; *Miscellaneous Observations,* I, 598; *Justification by Faith Alone,* IV, 75.

39. *God's Sovereignty,* IV, 52; *Miscellaneous Observations,* I, 604, 606.

40. *Wisdom Displayed in Salvation,* IV, 151.
41. *Miscellaneous Observations,* I, 603.
42. *Excellency of Christ,* IV, 189.
43. *Excellency of Christ,* IV, 179-201.
44. *Work of Redemption,* I, 404; *Wisdom Displayed in Salvation,* IV, 138.
45. *Justification by Faith Alone,* IV, 66, 95; *Decrees and Election,* II, 536; *Work of Redemption,* I, 431, 432.
46. *Justification by Faith Alone,* IV, 92.
47. *Justification by Faith Alone,* IV, 91.
48. *Work of Redemption,* I, 401, 402.
49. *Work of Redemption,* I, 403.
50. *Justification by Faith Alone,* IV, 98.
51. *Justification by Faith Alone,* IV, 65. Capitals in original.
52. *Wisdom Displayed in Salvation,* IV, 152.
53. *Pressing into the Kingdom of God,* IV, 381-402; *Ruth's Resolution,* IV, 412, 421.
54. *Miscellaneous Observations,* I, 595.

CHAPTER 2

1. Joseph Bellamy, *The Works of Joseph Bellamy, D. D. Late of Bethlem, Connecticut,* in three volumes. (New York: Stephen Dodge, Vols. I and II, 1811; Vol. III, 1812), II, 340, 341. (All citations from this source hereinafter will be taken from this edition and referred to as *Works.*)
2. Bellamy, *Works,* II, 539
3. Bellamy, *Works,* II, 529; see also I, 325.
4. Bellamy, *Works,* I, 197, 353. Note: Bellamy says that the gospel, too, is a "transcript of God." I, 374.
5. Bellamy, *Works,* I, 109, 112, 113, 121, 146, 320-322, 372, 373; II, 275, 376, 385, 380; III, 73, 79, 275.
6. Bellamy, *Works,* I, 347; see also I, 365, 366; II, 219, 220.
7. Bellamy, *Works,* I, 120, 147, 346, 347, 365, 366; II, 413-422.
8. Bellamy, *Works,* II, 540.
9. Bellamy, *Works,* I, 379.
10. Bellamy, *Works,* I, 83, 84, 487.
11. Bellamy, *Works,* I, 381.
12. *The Atonement. Discourses and Treatises by Edwards, Smalley, Maxcy, Emmons, Griffin, Burge, and Weeks. With an Introductory Essay*

by Edwards A. Park. Boston: Congregational Board of Publication, 1859. (All Citations from this source hereinafter will be taken from this edition and referred to as *The Atonement.*)

13. Quoted by Bellamy, *Works,* II, 414.
14. Bellamy, *Works,* I, 443, 431.
15. Bellamy, *Works,* III, 16f; III, 60-62.
16. Bellamy, *Works,* II, 381; see also I, 378.
17. Bellamy, *Works,* II, 369
18. Bellamy, *Works,* I, 390, 332.

CHAPTER 3

1. *Sketches of the Life of the Late Reverend Samuel Hopkins, D.D., an Autobiography* (Hartford: Hudson and Goodwin, 1805), p. 23f.
2. Park, *The Atonement,* p. lxii.
3. Samuel Hopkins, *The System of Doctrines, Contained in Divine Revelation, Explained and Defended. Shewing Their Consistency and Connection with each other. To which is added, A Treatise on the Millennium.* Second edition. (Boston: Lincoln and Edmands, 1811.), 2 Vols., I, 395. (Hereinafter referred to as *System*).
4. Hopkins, *System,* I, 396.
5. Hopkins, *System,* I, 321.
6. Hopkins, *System,* I, 449.
7. Hopkins, *System,* I, 85, 88.
8. Hopkins, *System,* I, 111; see also *System,* I, 121.
9. Hopkins, *System,* I, 118; see also I, 121.
10. Hopkins, *System,* I, 119, 120.
11. Hopkins, *System,* I, 121, 122.
12. Hopkins, *System,* I, 124, 125.
13. Hopkins, *System,* II, 143; see also II, 142-167.
14. Hopkins, *System,* I, 451-460.
15. Hopkins, *System,* I, 395.
16. Hopkins, *System,* I, 396.
17. Hopkins, *System,* I, 398, 399; see also I, 313.
18. Hopkins, *System,* I, 423f, 431f. The other two parts are His vicarious obedience and the completion of the salvation of those whom He redeems.
19. Hopkins, *System,* I, 399.
20. Hopkins, *System,* I, 403, 404.
21. Hopkins, *System,* I, 408.

22. Hopkins, *System,* I, 409.
23. Hopkins, *System,* I, 411; see also I, 388.
24. Hopkins, *System,* I, 412.
25. Hopkins, *System,* I, 417.
26. Hopkins, *System,* I, 404.
27. Hopkins, *System,* I, 397.
28. Hopkins, *System,* I, 422.
29. Hopkins, *System,* I, 422.
30. The expression, "covenant-transaction," is used by Edwards, Bellamy and Hopkins. The ontological implication is noteworthy. Hopkins holds that an eternal agreement existed between the Father and the Son respecting the Atonement. Hopkins explicitly says that the ancient doctrine of the Trinity is clearly taught in the Scripture but his treatment of that doctrine seems to be tri-theistic. This is not surprising, given his insistence upon the mutual agreement between the Father and Son. "Had there not been a God subsisting in three persons, so distinct as to covenant with each other, and act a separate and distinct part in the work of redemption, man could not have been redeemed, and there could have been no Redeemer." *System,* I, 387; see also 78, 82, 83.
31. Hopkins, *System,* I, 427, 428.
32. Hopkins, *System,* I, 452, 461; II, 72.

CHAPTER 4

1. Park, *The Atonement,* pp. lxv, lxvi.
2. Stephen West, *The Scripture Doctrine of Atonement,* second edition with appendix (Stockbridge; The Herald Office, 1809). (The Preface to the first edition is dated April 14, 1785). (Hereinafter referred to as *Doctrine of Atonement*).
3. West, *Doctrine of Atonement,* p. 66; see also *Doctrine of Atonement,* pp. 23, 25, 88, 112, 114, 150, 153.
4. West, *Doctrine of Atonement,* p. 66.
5. West, *Doctrine of Atonement,* p. 23.
6. West, *Doctrine of Atonement,* p. 158.
7. West, *Doctrine of Atonement,* p. 34.
8. West, *Doctrine of Atonement,* pp. 60, 61.
9. West, *Doctrine of Atonement,* p. 66.
10. West, *Doctrine of Atonement,* p. 107.
11. West, *Doctrine of Atonement,* p. 111.
12. West, *Doctrine of Atonement,* p. 104.

13. Park, *The Atonement,* p. lxxiii.
14. West, *Doctrine of Atonement,* p. 140.

CHAPTER 5

1. For a history of Universalism in America, see Richard Eddy, *Universalism in America. A History* (Boston: Universalist Publishing House, 1891). Two volumes. I., p. 211.
2. See Frank Hugh Foster, *A Genetic History of the New England Theology.* (Chicago: The University of Chicago Press, 1907). p. 190.
3. Foster, *A Genetic History of the New England Theology,* p. 190.
4. Joseph Haroutunian, *Piety Versus Moralism.* (New York: Henry Holt and Company, 1932), pp. 163, 164.
5. George P. Fisher, *History of Christian Doctrine,* (New York: Charles Scribner's Sons, 1896), p. 437. See also Foster, *A Genetic History of the New England Theology,* p. 191.
6. Williston Walker, *A History of the Congregational Churches in the United States. The American Church History Series* (New York: The Christian Literature Company, 1894, vol. III), p. 297.
7. Park, *The Atonement.*
8. Park, *The Atonement,* pp. lxxviii-lxxx.
9. Nathanael Emmons, "Necessity of the Atonement" in Park, *The Atonement,* p. 116.
10. Edwards A. Park, *Discourses on some Theological Doctrines as Related to the Religious Character* (Andover: Warren F. Draper, 1885), p. 180. (This work will hereinafter be cited as Park, *Discourses.*)
11. Maxcy, in Park, *The Atonement,* p. 95.
12. Park, *Discourses,* p. 167.
13. Smalley, in Park, *The Atonement,* p. 69.
14. Frank Hugh Foster, "New England Theology," *The New Schaff-Herzog Encyclopedia of Religious Knowledge,* edited by Samuel Macauley Jackson (New York: Funk and Wagnalls Company, 1910), VIII, 134.
15. Griffin, in Park, *The Atonement,* p. 165.
16. Fisher, *History of Christian Doctrine,* pp. 412, 413.
17. Maxcy in Park, *The Atonement,* p. 95. See also Doctor Edwards, in Park, *The Atonement,* pp. 9, 13; Griffin, in Park, *The Atonement,* pp. 264-266; Weeks, in Park, *The Atonement,* pp. 554, 555.
18. Doctor Edwards, in Park, *The Atonement,* 13.
19. Burge, in Park, *The Atonement,* 443, 444.
20. Burge, in Park, *The Atonement,* 442, 443.

21. Smalley, in Park, *The Atonement,* 58.
22. Doctor Edwards, in Park, *The Atonement,* 30.
23. Burge, in Park, *The Atonement,* 518.
24. Emmons, in Park, *The Atonement,* 115.
25. Burge, in Park, *The Atonement,* 519.
26. Doctor Edwards, in Park, *The Atonement,* 6.
27. Maxcy, in Park, *The Atonement,* 89.
28. Smalley, in Park, *The Atonement,* 54.
29. Weeks, in Park, *The Atonement,* 570.
30. Smalley, in Park, *The Atonement,* 70, 71.
31. Burge, in Park, *The Atonement,* 539. See also Doctor Edwards, in Park, *The Atonement,* 9; Maxcy, in Park, *The Atonement,* 100.
32. Griffin, in Park, *The Atonement,* 275.
33. Emmons, in Park, *The Atonement,* 128. See also Doctor Edwards, in Park, *The Atonement,* 33, 34; Smalley, in Park, *The Atonement,* 54.
34. Doctor Edwards, in Park, *The Atonement,* 35, 36.
35. Smalley, in Park, *The Atonement,* 81.
36. Emmons, in Park, *The Atonement,* 119.
37. Burge, in Park, *The Atonement,* 526.

A SELECT BIBLIOGRAPHY

A. Primary Sources

Bellamy, Joseph. *The Works of Joseph Bellamy, D. D. Late of Bethlem, Connecticut. In Three Volumes.* New York: Stephen Dodge, vols. I and II, 1811; vol. III, 1812.

Burge, Caleb. "An Essay on the Scripture Doctrine of Atonement, showing its Nature, its Necessity, and its Extent." See Park, *The Atonement.*

Dwight, Timothy. *Theology, Explained and Defended, in a Series of Sermons with a Memoir of the Life of the Author.* London: William Baynes and Son, 1824. vol. II. Five volumes.

Edwards, Jonathan. *The Works of President Edwards.* New York: Robert Carter and Brothers, 1881. Four volumes.

Edwards, Jonathan, Jr. *The Works of Jonathan Edwards, D. D. Late President of Union College. With a Memoir of His Life by Tryon Edwards.* Andover: Allen, Morrill & Wardwell, 1842. Two volumes.

———. "The Atonement Consistent with Free Grace." See Park, *The Atonement.*

Emmons, Nathanael. *The Works of Nathanael Emmons, with a Memoir of His Life written by Himself.* Boston: Crocker & Brewster, 1842. Six volumes.

———. "Necessity of the Atonement." See Park, *The Atonement.*

Griffin, Edward D. *A Series of Lectures, Delivered at Park Street Church, Boston, on Sabbath Evening*. Second edition. Boston: Nathaniel Willis, 1813

———. "An Humble Attempt to Reconcile the Differences of Christians Respecting the Extent of the Atonement." See Park, *The Atonement.*

Grotius, Hugo. *A Defence of the Catholic Faith concerning the Satisfaction of Christ, against Faustus Socinus.* (Translated with Notes and an Historical Introduction, by Frank Hugh Foster.) Andover: Warren F. Draper. 1899.

Hopkins, Samuel. *The System of Doctrines, Contained in Divine Revelation, Explained and Defended. Shewing Their Consistency and Connection with each other. To which is Added, A Treatise on the Millennium.* Second edition. Boston: Lincoln & Edmands, 1811. Two volumes.

———. *The Works of Samuel Hopkins, D. D. with a Memoir of His Life and Character by Edwards A. Park. Boston*: Doctrinal Tract and Book Society, 1852. Three volumes.

Maxcy, Jonathan. "A Discourse designed to explain the Doctrine of the Atonement." See Park, *The Atonement.*

Park, Edwards A. *The Atonement. Discourses and Treatises by Edwards, Smalley, Maxcy, Emmons, Griffin, Burge, and Weeks. With an Introductory Essay by Edwards A. Park.* Boston: Congregational Board of Publication, 1859.

Smalley, John. "Justification Through Christ, an Act of Free Grace." See Park, *The Atonement.*

Weeks, William R. "A Dialogue on the Atonement." See

Park, *The Atonement.*

West, Stephen. *An Essay on Moral Agency: Containing Remarks on a late anonymous Publication, entitled, An Examination of the late President Edwards's Inquiry on Freedom of Will.* (Second edition.) Salem: Thomas C. Cushing, 1794.

———. *The Scripture Doctrine of Atonement Proposed to Careful Examination.* (Second edition, with appendix.) Stockbridge: Printed at the Herald Office, 1809.

B. Secondary Sources

Allen, Alexander V. G. *Jonathan Edwards*. Boston: Houghton, Mifflin and Company,1890.

Boardman, George Nye. *A History of New England Theology*. New York: A. D. F. Randolph Company, 1899.

Brook, V. J. K. "The Atonement in Reformation and Post-Reformation Theology." *The Atonement in History and in Life.* (Edited by L. W. Grensted.) New York: The Macmillan Company, 1929.

Clarke, William Newton. *An Outline of Christian Thought.* Edinburgh: T. and T. Clark, 1911.

Cunningham, Charles E. *Timothy Dwight* 1752-1817, *a Biography*. New York: The Macmillan Company, 1942.

Eddy, Richard. *Universalism in America. A History*. Boston: Universalist Publishing House, 1891, vol. I. Two volumes.

Faust, Clarence H. and Thomas H. Johnson. *Jonathan Edwards. Representative Selections, with Introduction, Bibliography, and Notes.* New York: American Book Company, 1935.

Fisher, George P. *Discussions in History and Theology*. New York: Charles Scribner's Sons, 1880.

Foster, Frank Hugh. *A Genetic History of the New England Theology*. Chicago: The University of Chicago Press, 1907.

Haroutunian, Joseph. *Piety Versus Moralism*. New York: Henry Holt and Company, 1932.

Johnson, Thomas H. *The Printed Writings of Jonathan Edwards* 1703-1758: *A Bibliography*. Princeton: University Press, 1940.

Mackintosh, Hugh Ross. *The Christian Experience of Forgiveness*. New York: Harper and Brothers, 1927.

McGiffert, A. C. *A History of Christian Thought*. New York: Charles Scribner's Sons, 1932, vol. I; 1933, vol. II. Two volumes.

Miller, Perry. *Orthodoxy in Massachusetts*. Cambridge: Harvard University Press, 1933.

———. *The New England Mind*. New York: The Macmillan Company, 1939.

Mode, Peter G. *Source Book and Bibliographical Guide for American Church History*. Mensha: George Banta Publishing Company, 1921.

Parkes, Henry B. *Jonathan Edwards, the Fiery Puritan*. New York: Minton, Balch, and Company, 1930.

Progressive Orthodoxy. *A Contribution to the Christian Interpretation of Christian Doctrines by the Editors of "The Andover Review."* Boston: Houghton, Mifflin and Company, 1892.

Rashdall, Hastings. *The Idea of Atonement in Christian Theology*. London: Macmillan and Company, Ltd., 1925.

Sabatier, Auguste. *The Doctrine of the Atonement and its Historical Evolution*. (Translated from the French by Victor Leuliette.) New York: G. P. Putnam's Sons, 1904.

Schneider, Herbert Wallace. *The Puritan Mind*. New York:

Henry Holt and Company, 1930.

Sweet, William Warren. *Makers of Christianity*. New York: Henry Holt and Company, 1937.

———. *Religion in Colonial America*. New York: Charles Scribner's Sons, 1942.

———. *The Story of Religion in America*. New York: Harper and Brothers, 1930.

The Atonement in History and in Life. A Volume of Essays. (Edited by L. W. Grensted. New York: The Macmillan Company, 1929.

Walker, Williston. "The Congregationalists." *A History of the Congregational Churches in the United States. The American Church History Series*. New York: The Christian Literature Co., 1894, vol. III. Thirteen volumes.

———. *Great Men of the Christian Church*. Chicago: The University of Chicago Press, 1908.

———. *Ten New England Leaders*. New York: Silver, Burdett and Company, 1901.

Winslow, Ola Elizabeth. *Jonathan Edwards* 1703-1758. New York: The Macmillan Company, 1927.